Ten Myths About the Jews

Ten Myths About the Jews

MARIA LUIZA TUCCI CARNEIRO

Translated from the Portuguese by Carol Colffield

sussex
ACADEMIC
PRESS
Brighton • Chicago • Toronto

2 4 6 8 10 9 7 5 3 1

First published in 2020 in Great Britain by
SUSSEX ACADEMIC PRESS
PO Box 139
Eastbourne BN24 9BP

Distributed in North America by
SUSSEX ACADEMIC PRESS
Independent Publishers Group
814 N, Franklin Street
Chicago, IL 60610

British Library Cataloguing in Publication Data
A CIP catalogue record for this book is available from the British Library.

Library of Congress Cataloging-in-Publication Data
To be applied for.

Paperback ISBN 978-1-78976-047-7

Printed by TJ International, Padstow, Cornwall, UK.

Contents

Foreword

Ten Myths about the Jews

This study of anti-Semitism and the myths that feed it has been carried out and published at a time when – contrary to what was expected after the Holocaust, the establishment of the United Nations, the foundation of the State of Israel, the creation of the European Union and the end of the Cold War, as well as serious advances in the implementation of human rights – racism in its many forms pervades world society. The anticipation was that it would become a marginal phenomena or simply disappear is now lost, and needs to be redeemed. We are witnessing new forms of racism throughout the world, and one virulent form is anti-Semitism that makes wide use of myths about the Jews. The result is increased acts of violence against individuals and Jewish groups, irrespective of whether they live in authoritarian or democratic countries, or their economic situation. Israel's international standing, the persistence of the Arab–Israeli/Palestinian–Israeli conflict, and the advent of radical Islam against Jews, Zionism and the Israeli state provide a mixed bag of anti-Semitic motives. Legitimate criticism of Israeli government policy is used illegitimately as a means to argue that there should not be a Jewish state.

The current increase in anti-Semitism in contemporary Europe led Joel Kotkin, a distinguished commentator on international social trends, to write:

> Last month the German commissioner for "Jewish Life in Germany and the Fight Against Antisemitism" used his impressively titled office to advise German Jews against wearing kipahs in public. The commissioner's response to a surge of anti-Semitic violence in his country was a sheepish acknowledgment that Germany is once again a dangerous country for Jews. And as Germany goes, so goes Europe. For millennia, following the destruction of the Second Temple and the beginning of the diaspora, Europe was home to the majority of the world's Jews. That chapter of history is over. The continent is fast becoming a land of Jewish ghost towns and graveyards where the few remaining Jews must either accept an embattled existence or else prepare to leave.*

What does this mean in practice? No less than the countries that saw anti-Semitism emerge and develop over the centuries have not only failed to uproot it, but the resurgence of the phenomenon is increasing pressures that, through emigration and assimilation, markedly diminish the European Jewish presence and this despite historic Jewish contributions in many fields of science, literature, medicine, and humanistic endeavour.

It is against this background that the Brazilian historian María Luiza Tucci Carneiro presents an analysis of the appearance and development of ten myths about the Jews that have impacted on Jewish life and the societies in which they have lived for more than twenty centuries, in Europe and the rest of the world.

* Joel Kotkin "Judenrein Europe," *Tablet Magazine*, June 26, 2019, at https://www.tabletmag.com/jewish-news-and-politics/europe/286878/judenrein-europe, consulted on July 4, 2019.

The author uses the analytical structure of Raoul Girardet's political myths, which were preceded by Georges Sorel's theories on the mobilizing of myths and those of Gustave Le Bon on the impact of myths and the rhetorical and propaganda techniques that contributed so much to the genesis and the development of European Fascism, more than a century ago. The inaccuracy of the myth, and its encompassing force of simplicity, allow it to rapidly reproduce and adapt to different circumstances and societies; indeed, myths withstand the onslaught of time and adapt to social, economic and political changes. Based on the basic myth of Christian anti-Semitism that holds that the Jews killed Christ, and in the image of Judas Iscariot as the embodiment of treason, the author lists three social myths that hold that the Jews form secret groups against the common good; that the Jews are racist; and that they control the media. To these she adds the historical social myth of Jews without a country, wandering by nature and therefore lacking political and social loyalty to their places of origin or the societies that receive them. The economic myths speak about the domination that the Jews exert over the world economy; the fact that there are no poor Jews; that Jews are greedy by nature; that like parasites they exploit the societies in which they live. Finally, the political myth that holds that the Jews manipulate the economy of the United States of North America completes a very dark picture. The fact that the myths are interspersed and mixed gives them the kind of flexibility that allows them to withstand geographic change; thus myths of a totally European nature have appeared in societies as far away as Thailand and Japan – countries with minimal Jewish presence.

Ten Myths about Jews takes us, from the myth origins, generally European, to where Jews have migrated to. We shall learn how these myths have taken root in the Americas, and in particular Brazil, where the author's research has previously focused in her scholastic writings. The translocation of the myths, led by European conquerors and their institutions, highlights the nature of the interethnic mix of the American population, in the South and North, and the circumstantial fertility for the growth and proliferation of these beliefs.

Tucci Carneiro develops in an orderly fashion the historical investigation of each one of the myths presented, from its origins up to the present, accentuating the fact that the presentation of contradictory truths that prove the falsity of each one of the myths does not affect its impact on large segments of society. Paintings, pamphlets, cartoons and other visual manifestations illustrate the text; they serve to emphasize and confirm the scope, gravity and delegitimizing force of these myths with respect to the Jews as well as their potential toward promoting anti-Semitic social violence. *Ten Myths about Jews* is, in this period of history, a necessary reading to unravel not only anti-Semitism but the true nature of racism, which continues to affect so many segments of humanity despite the catastrophic lessons that should have been learned from history.

MARIO SZNAJDER
Professor Emeritus – The Hebrew University of Jerusalem

Representation of the Myth Iconography

Every effort has been made to identify, locate and contact all rightsholders for third-party illustrations used in this publication. If notified of any omissions or mistakes, the publisher will revise the source information at the earliest opportunity. Source information for the illustrations is provided in the text captions; the list below provides title information. The cover illustrations are nos 27 and 22.

Introduction

Ten Myths about the Jews invites readers to a journey into the collective imagination and reflection about a reality marked by racism. This book, which contains some of the main myths about the Jews, has been organized as a breviary, as a compendium of short texts that can be read in homeopathic doses. Although the myths are numbered there is no mandatory sequence because this is how myths are: each one has its own life. They become intertwined, superimposed as scales or tiles, and are united by deep roots originated in the substrate built from generation to generation. Because they appear to be true, they have as an attribute the verisimilitude to a reality that carries an appearance or likelihood of being true. Hence, the high level of conviction of a myth that, nourished by popular and scholarly culture, in fact, deceives.

I believe this is a provocative book, because it reconstitutes big lies with which we live in our everyday lives, although it is not always possible to be aware of their origins and purposes. But then comes the question: why and how do myths survive? First, it is important to clarify the concept of myth as it is used in this breviary: the purpose here is not to deal with myths whose narratives seek to explain phenomena of nature, the origins of man and womankind and the world, neither is it to make use of imaginary figures of gods, demigods and heroes, following the example of the mythologies from ancient Greek or Roman civilizations. The intention is not to discuss folkloric myths, myths of origin and distinction, founding myths or religious myths. Our object, at this moment, are the political myths about the Jews, their circulation and repercussion in contemporary societies and, especially, those that persist and instigate hatred against Jews. Myths about blacks, gypsies, indigenous people etc., could also be similarly reconstituted in another breviary.

Historian Raoul Girardet says that political myths are "like the dream that organizes itself into a dynamic of images [...] that chain themselves, are born from each other, call one another, talk to one another and become intertwined by means of a complex game of visual associations". In short: their contours are imprecise, "they overlap, interpenetrate and sometimes lose themselves within each other", as if they were bound by a subtle and powerful network of links of complementarity that "never ceases to keep passages, transitions and transferences among them".[1]

A political myth is not simply a social phenomenon or an idea. It is much more: it is the representation that is made of certain phenomena, people or ideas, which in turn generates a lie that will be eventually used as a truth. The myth is elaborated, modeled, with the purpose of "making people believe"; it is built with the intention of deceiving certain groups that trust what they hear or think they can see. The myth lies and manages to keep itself alive through constant repetition and re-elaboration of its own narrative, which is invariably seductive and full of details. Thus, for a thorough understanding of the myths that govern secular and ubiquitous antisemitism we analyze here ten narratives that tell different stories about the Jews which embody the myth and provide substance to it. Because it has persisted for centuries, the myth is also History, since a pseudo knowledge has been built with the purpose of sanctioning the version of those who, based on vested interests,

1 Raoul Girardet, *Mythes et mythologies politiques*, Paris, Seuil, 1990.

insist on the idea that Jews are an undesirable race or group. Those "marks" contribute to compose a distorted image of the Jewish people in their entirety, outlined through unsightly, diabolical, terrifying and antisocial figures. Common sense ignores the existence of a Jewish community fully integrated into society, multicultural and entrepreneurial (in trade, industry etc.), and present in multiple fields such as medicine, literature, philosophy and the arts, to name but a few examples.

A set of symbolic and mythical elements are constantly activated through the media and in oral tradition, keeping alive a lie that increasingly gains projection in a globalized world. For centuries, a "I have heard" attitude has contributed to unleash a succession of false images that explore the unconscious foundations of collective beliefs.

In general, the myth – which is polymorphic, dynamic, invisible and multifaceted – adapts itself to a fertile terrain excavated by ignorance and conquers new followers who, in the future, are going to, in turn, promote the myth. It is a commonplace – as can be seen in the documents left by the myth – that the narrative is combined with regional traditions that offer elements inspired by reality, and favor belief in those lies. This fact shows the persistence of totalitarian practices that, in the 1930s and 1940s, inspired the construction of "demons" and world conspiracies that certainly, at that time, contributed to speeding up many of the genocidal plans articulated by Nazi Germany. "Hitlerian demons" are still alive and show multiple facets, determined by representations that keep them in the agenda.[2]

2 On this subject I refer here to the important studies of Leon Poliakov, among them: *La causalité diabolique*, Paris, Calmann-Lévy, 1994; *Le mythe arien: Essai sur les sources du racisme et les nationalismes*, Paris, Calmann-Lévy, 1994.

Considering the political myth as one of the factors responsible for a radicalization of the racist thought in several countries around the world, it is important to analyze how a discourse that instigates hatred against the Jews and Israel is constructed. By focusing on the dynamics of political myths, we seek to explain here their genesis, transformation and proliferation, generally led by different voices. Voices that are present in our daily lives, but are difficult to identify because this is exactly one of the capabilities of the myth: it metamorphoses like a virus, with no possible diagnosis. It is up to us to denounce it, looking for convergence lines that can lead to those who produce it and are active subjects of violence and hatred towards the Other. Many times, myths circulate as a peripheral culture, and are interpreted as naïve, devoid of any killer intent. However, when evaluated in their entirety they can bring serious consequences for human beings, as was the case during the Nazi era.

In this breviary we analyze only ten of the myths against the Jews. There are many others; some are also secular and not just about Jews. In this group of social outcasts we include the gypsies, the blacks, indigenous people, homosexuals, and many other outsider groups. Hence, the concern to investigate the roots of the myths that persist under the bias of modernity and collective memory. By detecting the top ten myths about the Jews that circulate in the contemporary world, we are also questioning how and why such mental changes, fueled by lies and/or distortions, are processed.

Due to its historical roots, antisemitism is the result of the myth that, *par excellence*, is capable of disfiguring reality and of metamorphosing itself to take advantage of moments of acute crisis in which values must be (re)ordered. By analyzing the focus of this social and political phenomenon, we can identify the different forms of myths that coexist in a given society, which vary in terms of foundations and intensities. Lies, exaggerations, generalizations and distortions of historical facts emerge with the intention of inciting hatred against Jews. Hence the circulation of multiple imbricated "versions" that become increasingly latent and sharpened by the crisis in the Middle East, by the political reaffirmation of extreme right-wing groups or terrorist groups that defend programs aimed at excluding or destroying Israel and the Jewish people through violence, whether physical or symbolic.

By considering that the myth supports historical antisemitism, I stress that its narrative is always accusatory, steeped in stigma. For each version of the lie, the process of constructing the myth is reinforced over time based on a set of other narratives, whose dynamics include the myth of the heretic, of the wandering Jew, the pure "race", the "barbaric, false and hypocritical" people, the invading people and several other similar. Among the most common myths that contribute to reinforce antisemitic versions are: the Jews "dominate the world economy", "they act like a secret society", "they killed Jesus Christ", "there are no poor Jews", "they control the media", "they are racist", "they consider themselves superior", "they are greedy", "they do not want to integrate into the societies in which they live", "they are landless and homeless", and "they manipulate the United States"; to mention the most common ones…

Sources That Promote the Myth

The narratives of myths about Jews have in common an accusatory tone, that always insists on the idea that Jews are guilty and/or responsible for some crime, with or without violence. In short: in critical times, when values are being (re)ordered, Jews emerge as "scapegoats", the target-enemy, an image that continues to be fed even when normalcy is restored.

They are disqualified due to their culture; they are assaulted, physically or symbolically by means of slogans based on an antisemitic discourse. Throughout history, several other minorities or marginalized groups have also been used as "scape-goats" for some misfortune or failure: Jews are not the only ones. The myths that circulate about Afro-descendants and Gypsies are equally obnoxious

It is evident – from Antiquity up to the present – that someone must answer for the "evils that afflict the nation", an expression applied, for example, during the proliferation of the *Black Death,* a worldwide pandemic that killed millions of people in Europe in the late Middle Ages (14th century). The same expression was also used by the Iberian Inquisition to accuse New Christians, and was present in the antisemitic propaganda idealized by Nazi Germany, which blamed the Jews for the tragedy that afflicted the German people after the end of World War I.

The concept of scapegoat, however, is older than imagined. It is rooted in the Jewish tradition itself, in the so-called *Day of Atonement*, as quoted in Leviticus 16:5–28. In that event, the Hebrews organized a series of rituals to purify their nation using two goats that, by drawing lots, would have different destinies. One of them would be sacrificed next to a bull and its blood would be used to mark the temple walls; the other – spared from ritual death – was given the mission of bearing the sins of the people of Israel who symbolically went to the head of the animal through Aaron's hands. Immediately, he would send the scape-goat away into the wilderness, which would then carry "all the iniquities of the children of Israel, and all the transgressions in all their sins" (Lev 16:21–22).[3]

By following the trajectory of the myths in contemporary societies we can see that, no matter who produces them, they are aimed at seizing a particular sort of knowledge (popular and/or scholarly) that, when adapted to their interests, offers multiple resonances. Those who discriminate, assume a nuclear position, by masking their interests, manipulating information and acting aggressively. The target audience is generally unaware of the origins of the accusations and their minds are apt to believe those lies that bear an appearance or probability of truth.

The myths about the Jews emerge simultaneously in various parts of the world, corroded by secular prejudices that carry the gall of intolerance in their entrails. For the hatred to escalate, one step is enough. Many of those lies are based on secularized versions, inherited from medieval superstitions, the Catholic doctrine, Nazi ideology, anti-Zionism and anti-Americanism. Anti-Zionism has been strengthened by the conflicts in the Middle East that involve the State of Israel and the Palestinians, and presents itself as a propitious realm to falsify and distort both Judaism and the history of the Jewish people, thus favoring the proliferation of antisemitism. Hence the importance of creating and defining the borders of a Palestinian State in order to establish peace in the Middle East.

Qualifying adjectives continue to be widely used to compose the image and character of Jews who are accused of being violent, treacherous, terrorists, Nazi monsters, ungrateful, manipulators of information, and interested only in earning money. The traditional "Jewish gold" plot, set off by traditional antisemitism with Catholic foundations, continues to emerge

3 King James Bible, Leviticus, 16:21, http://biblehub.com/leviticus/16-21.htm. Retrieved: May 30, 2018.

as a symbol of mediocrity, a fertile space for the proliferation of racism. Likewise, Jews continue to be accused by anti-Zionist and antisemitic groups of not having the right to a homeland, and so, having to live as "eternal wanderers". If the Iberian Inquisition treated Jews and new Christians as "infected races", bearers of an "impure blood", the Nazi State transformed them into a subhuman (*Untermensch*) species, without the right to a citizenship, wanderers without a homeland. Today, those images are revived by the media (at times ill-informed or abusive with regard to facts), by extreme right and extreme left groups. In other words, we see that the lie circulates independently of ideology: it only needs fertile ground.

When analyzing some of the documents produced by Brazilian diplomats on missions abroad between 1933 and 1945, we can find that many of them endorsed this lie, without contradicting it. From their texts emerges the image of the *proscribed and fugitive Jew* (deserter), both derogatory expressions used to refer to the undesirable Jew. They are only symbolic codes of communication, words loaded with subjectivity, lies that are reheated in dark times. But in any situation, either past or present, it is always understood that the figure marked by the stigma of being Jewish, whether observant or not, as someone who was expelled from a homeland that "was not his", and for that reason, must wander towards infinity. In 1938 diplomat Barros Pimentel, from the Brazilian legation in Bern, endorsed the myth and defined the Jews as "belonging to the entire humanity" which, in short, refers to the citizen of the world.[4]

4 Maria Luiza Tucci Carneiro, *Cidadão do Mundo. O Brasil diante do Holocausto e dos Refugiados do Nazifascismo*, São Paulo, Perspectiva, 2011. Also available in German: *Weltbürger: Brasilien und die Flüchtlinge des Nationalsozialismus (1933–1948)*, transl. Marlen Eckl. Berlin, Lit Verlag, 2014; and in French: *Citoyen du Monde. Le Brésil face à l'Holocauste et aux*

Multiplication of the Lie

For a better understanding of how a lie that has been alive for centuries multiplies, it is important to bear in mind that here we are dealing with the "construction of a devilish, evil image". Those are representations of the Jew or the Jewish people that use metaphorical images that preexisted in the collective imaginary. Mental images are transformed into visual images that are easily delineated by means caricatures, photography and fine arts, which are susceptible to manipulation. From those examples it is possible to realize how a sort of knowledge, guided by hate-producing centers, aims at carving minds. This knowledge – nurtured by its own reproduction now facilitated by a globalized media – serves to legitimize the power of groups interested in "sweeping Israel and the Jews off the map".

This is a knowledge full of stigma (both physical and of character) that, in the form of lies disguised as truth, reinforces the anti-aesthetic and anti-social image of the Jew. Until 1950, for example, Jews were depicted in cartoons as figures with a hooked nose, flat feet, bearded, dirty, and ridiculed for their foreign accent "ingrained" in the country where they live. With the increasingly notable presence of Orthodox Jews in large urban centers and specific neighborhoods of Israel, this image has been reclaimed, its goal being to identify the Jew as a "stranger". Pre-existing mental images in the collective imaginary are stimulators of intolerant, violent attitudes. Through repetition, those images reinforce versions (narratives), that strengthen symbols and affective resonances (of repulsion, hatred, physical aggression) and feed negative visions about the Other. Thus, when explanations for immediate problems (economic crises,

---

réfugiés juifs, victims du nazisme (1933–1948), transl. Marie-Jô Ferreira, Paris, L'Harmattan, 2016.

unemployment, professional success, urban violence) are not evident, it is then that lies start populating the collective imaginary, fitting "like a glove". They adhere, stick, grow like a leavened bread dough, full of bubbles about to burst. Through those openings, new "aliens", "ETs", angels and vampires are born, carrying images explored by the cinema and by fiction literature. Those are fundamentalisms and alternative philosophies that linger on lies to impose their versions on facts.

In short, the myth is a construction: it is organized by a succession of images that dynamically aims at (re)ordering the world or a certain society. If the collective imaginary of the population is rich in metaphorical images, for example, it will be much easier to consider it as true. Especially those who are usually misinformed, who have some mental imbalance, or are disillusioned with their socioeconomic status, become easy targets for the racist myths. They move quickly from observation to fanaticism and then to acute, chronic paranoia. They are interested in finding an answer to their personal or group problems, and let themselves be wrapped by fears and references from the past. They easily turn into individuals receptive to conspiracy and genocidal theories, and get lost in the uncertainties, nooks and crannies of a society in crisis.

Depending on where the lie circulates, there are variations of intensity and nuances; they even disregard the need for Jews to organize as a community. The myth meets all their needs. There is also the strength of the myth: it shows characters and scenes that you want to see even if they do not exist. Hence the constant references to plots, secret agreements, underground tunnels, rich fortunes and "Holocaust industries", although those are invisible to the eye. In the twentieth and twenty-first centuries we can say that the *Protocols of the Sages of Zion*, one of the greatest hoaxes in history, continues to fuel those myths in many parts of the world.[5] Thus, the myth grows through the individual's relationships with social groups, the media and political propaganda. It takes advantage of cultural elements of local realities and, like an invisible web, it composes a network of meanings based on which "the world order is entirely thought and explained", using here the debate opened by Eduardo Colombo, a scholar devoted to the study of social imaginary.[6]

In the case of Jews, there is fertile ground feeding the germination of myths about this community: Judaism itself, as it is the case for every religion, is modeled through rites that, when projected on the collective imaginary, can lead to distorted interpretations. One of the most important rituals of Judaism – the ceremony of circumcision (*Brit Milah*), for example– besides being an obligation for all Jewish parents, is also a *mitzvah*, an act of connection with God[7], usually performed by a *mohel* or a doctor, that is, a professional trained to carry out the surgical procedure. Performed on the eighth day after the child's birth, it is explained as the Covenant of Abraham, following the teachings of the Torah, in the Genesis, where it is described as the promise made to God that guarantees the continuity of the Jewish people. At that time, the baby gets his or her Hebrew name. But how can a *Brit Milah* ceremony nourish the myth? Because it implies a "covenant" that involves blood, it demands the "suffering" of a

---

5 For information on the multiplication and damage caused by the various versions of *The Protocols of the Elders of Zion*, I suggest: Maria Luiza Tucci Carneiro (org.), *O antissemitismo nas Américas. História e Memória*, foreword by Pilar Rahola, São Paulo, Edusp, 2007.

6 Eduardo Colombo, *El Imaginario Social*, transl. Bernard Weigel, Montevideo/Buenos Aires, Altamira/Nordan-Comunidad, 1993, p. 47.

7 *Mitzvah* means a commandment as well as a connection: to be connected to God. When a Jew fulfills a *mitzvah*, it is understood that he is expressing this (positive) connection.

newborn and is a ritual asserting the continuity of a group that, according to the logic ingrained in the myth, is strengthened to impose its power to the world.

On several occasions, for instance, the inquisitors of the Holy Office of Spain and Portugal interpreted the *Minyan*[8] (a gathering of ten Jewish adults over 13 years old), as a secret plot, carried out in hiding, allegedly aimed at attacking Christianity. Such situations are the forerunners of the Catholic obsessions with conspiracies; those were beliefs that, for centuries, fueled a hysterical passion for Manichean explanations that attribute to the "conspirator" Jew the machination of massacres, the dissemination of plagues and viruses, and even the responsibility for earthquakes and other major misfortunes. In the same direction, this logic is used in the *Protocols of the Elders of Zion* and in the Hitlerite discourse as seen on the front page of the Nazi publication, *Der Stürmer*. Its headline warns: "Ritual Murder / The Greatest Secret of World Judaism". The illustration on the text reproduces a medieval depiction of ritual murder and brings the following caption:

> In 1476 the Regensburg Jews murdered six boys. They drew their blood and killed them as martyrs. The judges found the bodies of the deceased in an underground space that belonged to the Jew Josfal. On an altar was a plate of stone splattered with blood.[9]

8 Certain Jewish rituals or prayers can only be performed in the presence of a congregation which, according to the *Torah*, must be attended by at least ten male adults who form the *Minyan*. There should be a *Minyan*, for example, to perform the *Brit Milah* ceremony, for the prayers of the *Kadish, Barechah, Kedushah,* for *Torah* readings, among others.

9 *Der Stürmer: Deutsches Wochenblatt zum Kampfe und die Wahrheit* – Julius Streicher, Nuremberg, May 1939, p. 1. United States Holocaust Memorial Museum, courtesy of Virginius Dabney. ID: Collections: 1990.29.33.

Preis 20 Pfennig

Ritualmord-Nummer

Der Stürmer

...sches Wochenblatt zum Kampfe um die Wahrheit

HERAUSGEBER: JULIUS STREICHER

Nummer 20	Nürnberg, im Mai 1939	17. Jahr 1939

Ritualmord

Das größte Geheimnis des Weltjudentums

Was ist ein Ritualmord? Heute tappt auch die sogenannte gebildete Schicht in Deutschland in dieser Frage nicht mehr völlig im Dunkeln herum. Der Nationalsozialismus hat dafür gesorgt, daß es in den Köpfen aller Deutschen zu dämmern beginnt. Am gründlichsten aber ist über den jüdischen Ritualmord die Bauernbevölkerung fast aller Länder unterrichtet. In Deutschland, in Polen, in Rußland, in Rumänien, in der Türkei, in der Slowakei, kurz in all den Ländern, in denen Juden schon seit langer Zeit sitzen, ist auch das Wissen über den Ritualmord vorhanden. Die Alten erzählen es den Jungen und diese berichten es wieder ihren Kindern und Kindeskindern. Sie berichten, daß die Juden ein Mördervolk sind. Daß sie nach dem Blute der Nichtjuden gieren. Daß sie gegen alle Nichtjuden einen unmenschlichen Haß empfinden. Und daß dieser Haß besonders beim jüdischen Purimfest und beim jüdischen Osterfest (Passah- oder Pesachfest) zum Ausbruch kommt. An diesen Festen ist es bei den Juden Brauch, daß sie, wo es ihnen möglich ist, Nichtjuden an sich locken, um sie umzubringen. Meist sind es beim Purimfest erwachsene Nichtjuden, die regelrecht geschlachtet werden. Zum jüdischen Osterfest aber mordet der Jude mit Vorliebe nichtjüdische Kinder. Diese mordet er in der denkbar grauenvollsten und entsetzlichsten Weise. Er knebelt und fesselt das Kind. Er zersticht und zerfleischt es am ganzen Körper. Er öffnet ihm die Adern. Er sammelt das Blut in Schalen. Er trinkt dieses Blut oder er verwendet es für „religiöse" Bräuche. Ein solcher Brauch wird auch am jüdischen Osterfest (Passahfest) ausgeübt. Der Jude mischt getrocknetes Blut der Nichtjuden in den Wein, den er trinkt. Und er mischt nichtjüdisches Blut in die „Mazzen" (ungesäuerte Brote), die er backt und zum Weine ißt.

SEX PVERI RATISPONÆ AB IVDÆIS INTERFECTI

Zu nebenstehendem Bild:

Im Jahre 1476 ermordeten die Juden in Regensburg sechs Knaben. Sie zapften ihnen das Blut ab und marterten sie zu Tode. Die Richter fanden in einem unterirdischen Gewölbe, das dem Juden Josfol gehörte, die Leichen der Ermordeten. Auf einem Altar stand eine mit Blut befleckte steinerne Schale.

Bild und Bericht aus dem Buch: „Bavaria Sancta", III. Band S. 174)

Die Juden sind unser Unglück!

1990.029.33

1. *Der Stürmer: Deutsches Wochenblatt zum Kampfe und die Wahrheit* – Julius Streicher, Nuremberg, May 1939, p. 1. United States Holocaust Memorial Museum, courtesy of Virginius Dabney. ID: Collections: 1990.29.33

In some updated editions of the same *Protocols*, published by *Editora Revisão*, a Brazilian publishing house, the Jewish presence has been linked to the proliferation of AIDS and drugs. Those examples demonstrate the ability of political myths to update themselves and survive on traces of the past. Hence the persistence of the "demonization" of the Jews as eternal "scapegoats".[10]

Construction of the "Jewish Danger"

Myths against ethnic minorities (Jews, Gypsies, Blacks, Native peoples, etc.) are dangerous because, by a dynamic of images that are chained together, they prepare minds to validate genocide or any other kind of physical or symbolic violence. They instigate "witch-hunting" movements and transform arguments into mobilizing forces. Many times, a fragment of reality is enough to detonate hatred, incite persecution, prisons, torture, deportations and massacres. The emotional charge becomes so strong that part of the population believes in lies, as was the case during the Iberian Inquisition period (Spain: 1478–1834; Portugal: 1536–1821) and the Nazi Era (1935–1945). It is known that the Catholic doctrine, as well as the totalitarian and authoritarian propaganda apparatuses, have contributed a great deal to the creation of "virtual" victims, speeding up the process of "demonization" of Jews who were treated as monsters, as a degenerate, inferior or infected race.[11] An expression of that is

10 León Poliakov, *La causalité diabolique: Essai sur l'origine des persécutions*, Paris, Calmann-Lévy, 1994.

11 Maria Luiza Tucci Carneiro, *Preconceito Racial em Portugal e Brasil Colônia. Os cristãos-novos e o mito da pureza de sangue*, 3rd ed., São Paulo, Perspectiva, 2004.

the antisemitic caricature published by Julius Streicher in his newspaper *Der Stürmer* in October 1937. The image depicts the Jew as the devil who threatens Mother Europe. The caption reads: "Mother Europe / If I had to leave one of my children to this demon, it would be my death".

I believe it is difficult to study and understand the history of antisemitism before evaluating a collective imaginary populated by archetypes that should neither be put aside or ignored. The stereotypical images about Jews that coexist there – wandering Jew, capitalist Jew, selfish Jew, degenerate Jew, murderous Jew, etc. – are responsible for generating forces that can alter the order within a society, as took place during the Portuguese colonial empire and Nazi Germany. Mythical stories favor the creation of heroes/saviors of the nation, the institution of hierarchies and models of social relations shaped by Manichaeism: one believes in the existence of a society divided between opposing forces: Good versus Evil.

Thus, myths are transformed into regulatory forces of a given society and serve to control the masses, a situation that is common either to absolutist, totalitarian or authoritarian regimes. Suffice it to say that, both in Spain (1478–1834) and Portugal (1536–1821), the Inquisition Court did not measure efforts to eliminate Jews and new Christians based on the concept of blood impurity, which was abolished only in the 19th century, as I have demonstrated in my studies on the subject.[12] In the same vein is the conclusion by Christiane Stallaert who considers that those details:

> [the elimination of Jews is] historically oriented towards a biological and cultural component such as was the *limpieza*

12 *Ibidem.*

> *de sangre* [blood cleansing] that was applied to *Jews, Moors, Moriscos, Marranos,* etc., with the purpose of rejecting them, of not integrating them in the society or of having against them, several precautions generated by mistrust. Christian hegemony is then imposed and with it, the Hispanic identity.[13]

In the case of Nazi Germany, Jews were classified by the national-socialist leaders as elements of "deviation" to the enacted order and of "degeneration" for the "purebred" German race; as such, they were to be exterminated. The myths helped to explain the "evils that plagued the German nation" and directed the behavior of a population that was predisposed to endorse the narrative/lie. By means of cartoons, films, radio, photography, children's books, parades and national anthems, the myth expanded and channeled the energies towards a consensus – the salvation of the German society depended on its leader (Adolf Hitler, the "savior") – and the division of the population into pure and impure, which culminated by the endorsement of genocidal practices.

According to Pierre Ansart, the myth "participates in the renewal of a certain order, in the institution of a certain hierarchy and, as a consequence, in the elimination of the dominated ones [read the outcasts]: the myth enhances the violence that, up to then, had been repressed, and thus becomes legitimized by the State".[14]

---

13 Review by Carlos Junquera Rubio on the work by Christiane Stallaert, *Etnogénesis y Etnicidad en España. Una aproximación histórico-antropológica al casticismo*, published in *Estudios del hombre*, n. 18, 2003, p. 215.

14 Pierre Ansart, "Ideologías, Conflitos e Poder", in Eduardo Colombo, *op. cit.*, pp. 101–102.

Deutsches Wochenblatt zum Kampfe um die Wahrheit

HERAUSGEBER: JULIUS STREICHER

Nummer 43		Nürnberg, im Oktober 1937		15. Jahr 1937

Judenstaat Palästina

Die Judenfrage ist die Schicksalsfrage des englischen Volkes

Der englische Plan

Die englische Regierung zerbricht sich über die Frage „Palästina" schon seit langer Zeit den Kopf. Sie möchte gerne den Streit beenden, der dort zwischen Juden und Arabern tobt. Sie hat darum einen Plan ausgearbeitet. Danach soll das Land Palästina geteilt werden. Einen Teil des Landes sollen die Juden erhalten, der andere Teil soll den Arabern zugesprochen werden. Mit dieser Teilung haben sich aber beide Völker nicht einverstanden erklärt. Die Araber lehnen die Teilung ab, weil sie das ganze Land für sich beanspruchen. Sie erklären, sie seien die eingesessene Bevölkerung und die Juden hätten ihnen einen Teil des Landes durch Betrug und Ausbeutung lediglich gestohlen. Die Juden lehnten den Plan überhaupt und von vornherein höhnisch und brüsk ab. Sie ließen den Engländern sagen, daß sie unter gar keinen Umständen auf solch eine lächerliche Landeszuteilung eingehen würden.

Wer nun die Karte ansieht und die Verhältnisse in Palästina einigermaßen kennt, der weiß, daß dieser englische Teilungsplan nichts anderes ist, als ein ungeheures Entgegenkommen der englischen Regierung gegenüber den Juden. Das Land Palästina ist außerordentlich fruchtbar in dem Teil, der sich der Küste entlangzieht. Dagegen ist es eine öde, sandige und felsige Wüste in seinem Innern. Ursprünglich besaßen die Araber alles Land und beackerten es. Die Juden waren früher auch in Palästina ebenso wie in anderen Ländern nichts anderes als Geldverleiher, Händler und Wechsler. Das heißt, sie lebten ebenso wie in anderen Ländern vom Wucher und vom Betrug. Als aber die Juden die zionistische Bewegung gründeten, begann sich in Palästina ein Wandel zu vollziehen. Besonders nach dem Kriege wanderten systematisch die Ju-

Aus dem Inhalt

Wenn Juda mordet
Gefährliche Jugendlektüre
Berliner Brief
Die Talmudbestien Nußbaum und Dr. Sulzberger / Vom Viehtreiber zum Hofbankier und Millionär
Am Juden zu Grunde gegangen

Mutter Europa

„Und sollte ich diesem Teufel nur eines meiner Kinder überlassen müssen, es wäre mein Tod"

Die Juden sind unser Unglück!

2. *Der Stürmer: The Devil Threatening Mother Europe*, Nuremberg [Bavaria, Germany], October 15, 1937. United States Holocaust Memorial Museum, courtesy of Gerard Gert. Available at: https://collections.ushmm.org/search/catalog/pa1120753. Access: 10.08.2019.

Renewal of the Myths by New Technologies

In the 21st century, it is important to evaluate the persistence and revitalization of political myths in light of new technologies and their impact on the construction of knowledge about the Jews. From a historical perspective we realize that myths, due to their dynamics and capacity for renewal, have moved from the medieval oral tradition to the modern means of mass communication. Today, updated, they spread faster through computers, software, interactive games, smart phones and the Internet. They incite hatred through global lies, without borders or identity, and are transmitted by neo-Nazi and antisemitic blogs. Backed by laws that protect freedom of speech and hidden behind the anonymity enabled by the Internet, bloggers appeal to this freedom to compose and illustrate their repertoire with mental and visual images inspired by the near past. Seduced by myths, they offer their readers a "kingdom of happiness".

By means of news stories on the Middle East that place Israel as the focus of political criticism, mythological narratives are brought up to date and help to inject insecurity and to amplify hatred against Jews and the State of Israel. Sensationalist media using the large power of photography as a document – truthfulness – intensify, as correctly stated by Gilles Lipovetsky, the possibilities "of a world full of catastrophes and dangers".[15] Appealing to emotion, photography favors the construction of a second reality[16] and strengthens the myth. The crisis of paradigms that shakes the 21st century opens up spaces for the circu-

15 Gilles Lipovetsky, *Metamorphoses de la culture libérale: éthique, médias, entreprise*, Montréal, Éditions Liber, 2002.

16 See Boris Kossoy, *Realidades e Ficções na Trama Fotográfica*, 5th ed. São Paulo, Ateliê Editorial, 2016.

lation and revitalization of myths. We cannot forget that the mind, using lies and distorting facts, is still a prisoner of the totalitarian logic.

From the point of view of the collective mentality, we can consider that the myth of the Judeo-Masonic international conspiracy continues today as one of the paradigms of modern antisemitism. At the same time, the millennial-long hatred against Jews survives, sponsored by media segments that feed distorted opinions about the crisis in the Middle East. As an example, following the terrorist attacks on the World Trade Center (New York) and the Pentagon, home of the United States Department of Defense (Washington, DC) on September 11th, 2001, some intellectuals, journalists and academics celebrated the act of terror with a dose of antisemitism. In other situations, by attempting to reveal the vulnerability of U.S. imperialism and accusing Israel of "terrorism" and "Nazi genocide" against the Palestinians, those citizens broke, once again, the snake's egg. Unfortunately, we are unable to go through the 21st century immune to this poison that still enchants the enemies of democracy.

The Ten Myths

MYTH 1

The Jews Killed Christ

The myth says that "the Jews killed Jesus Christ". This is one of the traditional accusations that make up the breviary of Christian and popular antisemitism. It is an expression that has never ceased to manifest itself in countries with a Catholic tradition. The truth is that such an accusation, initially, served the purposes of the pioneers of Christianity, who were interested in forging the evil image of the Jews, fueling a fear that was capable of distorting reality.

By transforming the Jews into Christ killers, Christian scholars tried to drown out the doubts cast by the Jews as to the earthly nature of Jesus, the illusory character of his resurrection and the claim that he was not the long-awaited Messiah.

Over the centuries, the myth that "the Jews killed Christ" was reaffirmed and renewed by other myths that, from the 12th century onwards, helped to strengthen the idea of the "Jewish danger" and to generate prejudiced popular beliefs. Such hostilities reached their peak in the period after the Crusades and the establishment of the Iberian Inquisition, when the Catholic Church strengthened the discourse of a "Christian unity" in their struggle against heretics. During the Middle Ages, for example, most people believed the legend of the ritual murder of a child – allegedly celebrated annually during Easter – the desecration of the hosts, the accusation that Jews poisoned wells. The attribution of those crimes to Jews has in common the idea that they were conspirators against Christianity and, as such, should be eliminated.

In its essence, the myth that "the Jews killed Christ" is rooted in interpretations of the Gospels by Christian scholars who instigated hatred and violence through their preaching. Over the centuries, this lie has circulated in Catholic catechisms, sermons, inquisitorial manuals, an abundant iconography, encyclopedia entries, drama texts, journalistic chronicles, *cordel* literature, political caricatures and the "useful" knowledge disseminated by illustrated magazines and almanacs. Secular, pastoral and clergy manuals, as well as Catholic and Protestant newspapers, have contributed to affirming the concept of a "deicidal crime" (the murders of God's and, Jesus Christ murder), presented here as a long-lasting myth. It originated in the Judeo-Christian polemics that, from the 1st to the 4th century, have promoted the distance between Christianity and Judaism, and are constantly revitalized by new mental and visual images.

This topic has already been deeply analyzed by several scholars, whose studies are references to understand the construction process of the *myth of the deicide Jew*, that persists and inserts itself in the mentality of people, influencing social behavior, since the Middle Ages. Among the historians dealing with this issue are Jules Isaac, Leon Poliakov, Cecil Roth, Robert M. Seltzer, Edward Flannery, Joshua Trachtenberg and Sérgio Alberto Feldman.[17] Taken together, their studies highlight two factors that have contributed to the persistence of the deicide

17 On this subject see: Jules Isaac, *Las Raíces Cristianas del Antisemitismo*, Buenos Aires, Paidos, 1966; Cecil Roth, *A Short History of the Jewish People, London*, Hartmore House, 1969; León Poliakov, *Du Christ aux Juifs de cour (Histoire de l'Antisémitisme)*, Paris, Calmann-Lévy, 1955; Robert M. Seltzer, *Jewish People, Jewish Thought: The Jewish Experience*

crime: the growing process of Christianity's de-judaization and the construction of an accusatory narrative by Christians interested in pointing the finger at a culprit for the crucifixion of Jesus Christ.

To understand this process that culminated in the demonization of the Jews as a symbol of evil, it is essential to go back in time in search of the genesis of this myth. Early anti-Jewish ideas can be identified in the Roman Empire, when the land was believed to be a flat disk and its boundaries were not far away. Violent accusations against Jews began inside the synagogues and continued in the preaching of the apostles who, like Jesus, were "dissenting Jews". Christian literature written in the 2nd and 3rd centuries already criticized Jews for not having accepted Christ's faith and for not having renounced their "old" rituals. Among the apostles we allude here to Paul of Tarsus who, in order to conquer new followers, encouraged people to break the commandments of the Jewish Law, renouncing to circumcision and to dietary restrictions.

Until the 30s and 40s CE, Jesus followers in Jerusalem still preached in the Temple, observed Jewish laws and saw themselves as members of the Jewish people, thus maintaining a "reasonable coexistence between Christians and Jews".[18] Even because Christians needed to be recognized by the Roman

in History, London, Pearson, 1980, 2 volumes; Joshua Trachtenberg, *El Diablo y los Judíos. La Concepción Medieval del Judío y su Relación con el Antisemitismo Moderno,* Buenos Aires, Paidos, 1975; Javier Domínguez Arribas, *El Enemigo Judeo-masónico en la Propaganda Franquista (1936–1945),* Madrid, Marcial Pons Editorial, 2009; Sérgio Alberto Feldman, "Deicida e Aliado: O Judeu na Patrística", in Academia.edu. http://www.academia.edu/1375074/Deicida_e_aliado_do_demonio_o_judeu_na_Patristica; Edward Flannery, *The Anguish of the Jews: Twenty-Three Centuries of Antisemitism,* New Jersey, Paulist Press, 2004.

18 León Poliakov, *op. cit.*, p. 17; Robert M. Seltzer, *op. cit.*, vol. I, p. 212.

Empire as members of a legitimate, consolidated and rooted religion – *religio licita* – a condition enjoyed by Jews, whose position was ancient. That was indeed one of the challenges that Christians had to face: to obtain the recognition of their religion as lawful by the Romans. However, in order to achieve such a status, they had to annul the Jewish conceptions, including the one that denied Christ as the Messiah. By insisting on that idea, the Jews created obstacles to the legitimation of Christians, who defended (and defend still today) the belief that Jesus was crucified, resurrected and, forty days later, ascended to heaven in front of his twelve apostles; then hereturned as the Redeemer, according to the descriptions of the New Testament (Luke 24:50–53; Mark 16:19; Acts I: 9–11).

Summarizing: from an initially cordial conduct, Christians gradually started to adopt an aggressive attitude, a situation that became more and more evident from 66 CE onwards, when the Jews of the land of Israel rebelled against Rome and were not supported by the group of Jew-Christians (baptized), accused of being traitors. In 132–135, after the second revolt of the Jews against Rome led by Shimon Bar-Kochba, the separation of Jews and Catholics became more evident, shaping the real impact of Christianity on Judaism. As a result, a repressive measure, one of the first antisemitic demonstrations from a state: two anti-Jewish edicts promulgated by Adrian in 135, that were revoked by his successor, Antonine, in 138.

The Holy Scriptures came to be interpreted differently on both sides and during the Middle Ages, they received additions and allegories from Christians that sought to define themselves as those who:

> [...] respected God and did not commit crimes. They did not accept the Golden Calf; they did not practice idolatry

> in the time of the Prophets and were faithful servants of God. That proto-Christianity was between the lines of the Elected People, it was its just and faithful part. They were the Hebrews. To that group belonged the Patriarchs, Moses, Joshua, David and the prophets. On the other hand, the worshipers of the Golden Calf, the idols of Baal and Astarte, the persecutors of the Prophets, would be the Jews. They lived with their just and faithful brethren, but collided with them throughout history. God, countless times, had warned them and ended up punishing them with exile. Next, they would be the ones who would not accept Christ and remain Jewish. The Hebrews already accept Christ and receive Gentiles into their bosom, becoming the true Israel. Thus, on the one hand, there are the Jews, an evil and unfaithful side; and on the other, the Hebrews, the just and faithful side of God who remains Christian.[19]

From that narrative, repeated in several other Christian texts,[20] the Jews, from being the "People of the Book" and the "People chosen by God", became the "Murderous People" and the "People chosen by Satan". Sérgio Feldman, in his magnificent article on the subject, analyzes the texts written by the founders of Catholicism, and demonstrates how the process of demonization of the Jews took place. Among the authors who argue about the "malignancy" of the Jews, the author cites: Eusebius, bishop of Caesarea, Hilary of Poitiers, John Chrysostom, Bishop of Antioch, Hieronymus, Augustine of Hippo, Isidore of Seville, who lived in Visigoth Hispania at the end of the 6th century and the beginning of the 7th century.

19 Sérgio Feldman, *op. cit.*, p. 7.

During the Early Middle Ages, thanks to Augustine's most tolerant preaching, the Jews of Western Europe managed to live with a certain tranquility and protection, being valued for their administrative, commercial and financial activities. From the 12th century onwards, the panorama was altered by virulent anti-Jewish discourses prepared by the Church's fathers, including John Chrysostom (344–407), Bishop of Antioch, and Isidore (560–636). Based on the Scriptures, Chrysostom claimed that:

> The synagogue would be a theater and a "center of prostitution", a house of thieves and lodging for wild beasts (Sermon 6:5). A place of shame and ridicule (1:13), the demon's abode (1:6), just as the Jewish soul is possessed by the demon; its rites are criminal and impure (3:1). These denunciations are interspersed with quotations from the biblical text, from which a rereading is done. Jews are described as corrupt and criminal beings. They are the *murderers of Christ* (6:1).[21]

Jerome, in turn, despite his close contact with rabbis and Jewish scholars in Palestine, did not alter the virulent tone of that discourse. In his opinion, the Jews were "serpents, haters of all men"; their image is that of Judas and the psalms and prayers are a "bray of donkey"; he assures that they curse Christians in the synagogues.[22]

---

20 *Idem.*

21 Cited by Sérgio Feldman, *op. cit.*, pp. 9–11 [italics added].

22 François de Fontette, *Histoire de l'Antisémitisme*, Paris, Presses Universitaires de France, Collection. Que Sais-Je?, 2015; Edward Flannery, *op. cit.*, p. 66, cited by Sérgio Feldman, *op. cit.*

The accusation that the Jews killed Christ became more and more rooted in Christianity and originates in the Jewish-Christian polemics that contributed to spread the slander between the 1st and 4th centuries. That process of defamation culminated in the demonization of Jews, who were encouraged to strengthen Christianity (presented as a symbol of Good) in opposition to Judaism (symbol of Evil). It is in that context that we look for explanations for the violence against Jews during the bubonic plague or Black Death as it became known, which affected several European countries, including France where *pogroms* occurred in 1348. On that occasion, Pope Clement VI promulgated two papal bulls that emphasized that the Jews were not guilty for the plague. He achieved no success, though. Under the leadership of the Count of Savoy, dozens of Jews were imprisoned and tortured in regions around Lake Geneva, accused of poisoning Christianity.

In other places, such as Basel, members of the Jewish community were accused of poisoning the wells, Jewish children were removed from their parents and forcibly converted to Christianity. It is estimated that about 600 Jews were handcuffed, caged, and immediately burned by the angry population. The situation was similar to that of about 2,000 Jews in Strasbourg, who were burned alive despite attempts to protect them by the bishop and the city council. *Pogroms* occurred in several towns and villages along the Rhine River, as well as in Erfurt, Germany, where 3,000 Jews were killed on charges of spreading the Black Plague. In Worms, four hundred Jews were burned in March 1349, and in Frankfurt part of the Jewish community opted for mass suicide rather than forced conversion. In short: at the height of the pandemic, between 1348 and 1351, since, when compared to other groups, much of the Jewish community had been shielded from the disease, the

3. *The Burning of Jews*. Illustration by Michael Wolgemut and Wilhelm Pleydenwurff, reproduced from Shedel, Hartmann, Liber Chronicarum, 1493, p. 533. Bavarian State Library/World Digital Library, https://www.wdl.org/en/item/410/. Access: 10.08.2019.

figure of the Jew served as a scapegoat. According to Martin Blaser from New York University, most Jews had not been contaminated by the disease because, following the precepts of Judaism, they kept their homes sanitized from impurities and their hands clean during meals.[23]

From the 14th century onwards, the Jews who lived in the Iberian Peninsula were also seen as a dangerous minority within Christianity, even though, up to then, they had shared the same spaces. That was the solution found by the absolutist State and the Iberian Catholic Church to solve conflicts between Christians and Jewish dealers, who, threatened by death penalty, were forced to convert to Catholicism, first in Spain (1391), then in Portugal (1492). By accusing the New Christians of being "members of an infectious race" and heretics, the State and the Church, in addition to seizing property that belonged to Jews, collaborated to prevent the rise of a Jewish bourgeois middle class who had become business competitors of the Old-Christians.

The establishment of the *Tribunal del Santo Oficio* in Spain (1478) and Portugal (1536), fostered a type of antisemitism of theological foundations that contributed to a long process of social and physical exclusion of the New Christians. The origins of this prejudice can be traced back to the enactment of the Judgment-Statute of Toledo, in 1449, which divided the Iberian

23 Cited by Donald G. MacNeil Jr., "As Epidemias e os Bodes-expiatórios", in Caderno "The New York Times", *Folha de S. Paulo*, Sept. 14, 2009.

Sexta etas mundi

Calamitosa gens hebreorum in oppido baioarie nomine deckendorff sito in littore danubij anno dñi.1337. maiestatē ihesu xp̄i i diuinissimo sacramento mirũmmodũ ɔtēpsit ⁊ religionem nostrā illusit. Id pᵒ varias punctiones in fornace ignis posuerũt illesum tñ ab igne māsit. in incude q̃z malleis pcusserũt. Qua re (diuino nutu) cognita prefectus oppidi hartmannᵒ de degēberg cũ ciuibus oppidi iudeoꝝ domᵒ inuaserunt. nō sexui. nō etati parcentes veritate cognita debit[illegible] penis afflixerũt ⁊ neci dederũt. Sacramētũ obseruatũ in eccĩa sepulchri dñi miraculis varijs i eo operātibus honoratur.

Iudei q̃z oēs qui in germania erāt deinde anno dñi.1348. videlicet tpe ɔbusti sunt. [illegible] omnis regionis puteos intoxicare fuerũt annixi vt multi eoꝝ ɔfessi sunt. perijsse aliq̃t milia ferunt ⁊

Locuste ac bestiole innumerabiles multiplicato numero ab oriente in occidentem instar dense nubis celũ obducentes vastarunt. herbas ⁊ omnes fructᵒ terre. q̃rũ corruptione ⁊ fetore execrabil' pestelētia subsecuta ē.

Pestis lugubris ⁊ miseranda hoc anno.1348. incepit ⁊ p tres annos p totũ pene orbē debaccata est. q̄ pmo in asiā apd indos ob easdē bestiolas incipiens passim p puincias irrepens vsq̃z in brittannos. Per mare igit anno sequēti irrepēs regna ytalie. postea francie ⁊ britannie. demũ germanie puincias ⁊ hungarie sua ɔtagione infecit. adeoq̃z deseuit apud omnes gentes vt vix decimus quisq̃z ex millesimo hoīe supfuerit. In aliq̃bus locis vix tercia ps hoīm remaneret. ⁊ pleraq̃z loca ne dũ campestria. verũ arces. oppida ⁊ vrbes psus derelicta sunt ac in solitudinem redacta.

Huic calamitati augmentum dedisse iudeos in fontium intoxicatione nonnulli arbitrati sunt.

Gerhardus ordinis heremitarum

Gerhardũ senensem ordĩs heremitaꝝ diui augustini sacraꝝ lraꝝ clarissimũ interpretem hac ipa tempestate admodũ senē obijsse tradũt. virũ vtiq̃z ingenij eminentissimũ ⁊ bti Egidij ro. imitatorē pcipuũ. q̄ cũ esset in sacra theologia doctus sup primũ sententiaꝝ accuratissime scripsit. Deinde tractatus de pscriptionibus ⁊ de vsucaptionibus ⁊ de vsuris ceterisq̃z ɔtractibᵒ opuscula edidit. quibᵒ diuᵒ bernhardinᵒ ɔterraneus suᵒ in tractatu suo restitutionũ plurimũ vsus ē. Hũc etiam tractatũ Jo. an. eiᵒ ɔtēporaneᵒ multis in locis ⁊ maxie mercurialibᵒ plurimũ ɔmēdat.

Gerhardᵒ itē eiusdē ordĩs ⁊ doctrine pfessor patria bergomēsis ⁊ sauonēsis eps eo tpe in pcio existēs pplo suo peste laborāti vt bonũ decet epm magis pdesse admixus ē q̃z pesse. q̄ cũ pontificij iuris edoctus esset in sextũ decretaliũ cōmentatus est. ⁊ multa in laudē sue religionis in lucē deduxit. q̄olibeta duo parisiᵒ disputauit ⁊ multa opuscula edidit. moriens deniq̃z nō sine sanctitatis noīe bergomi iuxta maius altare celebri sepulchro a se constructo sepelitur.

Thomas florētinᵒ medicᵒ diui q̄ndā medici filiᵒ hisdē tpibᵒ nō inferiori ingenio famaue patri subsecutus. etiā de arte medēdi sūmā pulchrā pᵒ se reliquit.

Bartolus legũ doctor

Bartolus saxoferrateus iuriscōsultoꝝ supioris seculi princeps ⁊ eiusdē pfessionis copiosissimus explanator. Cyni ⁊ iacobi bothigarij doctoꝝ discipulus ⁊ auditor. His q̃z temporibus vniuerso mundo (ea in doctrina) admirabilis fuit. Qui ⁊ p̄ ceteris legũ interptibus in digesto nouo ⁊ veteri. ac inforciato nec nō et in reliquis legũ codicibus pclarissima edidit cōmentaria. q̄z celebritate atq̃z pstantia ipe vulgatissimus habitᵒ ē. Scripsit ⁊ tyberiadis tractatus. ac alium de guelphis ⁊ gibellinis. Ferunt etiā eiᵒ pclara ɔsilioꝝ volumina. Obijt aũt anno dñi.1355. etatis vero quinquagesimosexto.

Franciscus quoq̃z albergotus natione aretinus solidus legum doctor ⁊ explanator bartoli amicissimᵒ et familiaris ac imitator quedam extantia composuit.

Jacobinᵒ carrariēsis q̄ marsiliũ interfecit h̄ anno postq̃z q̄tuor annis in patauio sceptra tenuisset. ⁊ ipe a guilielmo eius ex pelice filio interficit. cuiᵒ parricidij hec cā fuit q̄ ab eo ɔtumeliose spuriᵒ appellatus est. mox vt domum regressus est patrē in secreto accersiuit ⁊ gladio impetens eũ cōfodit. ⁊ statim in templo diui augustini eum sepeliri fecit. vt nō euacuet verbum xp̄i qui gladio feriet gladio pibit.

society into pure-blooded Old-Christians and New-Christians, considered members of a race infected by Jewish, Moorish, Gypsy or black blood. A new universe presented itself to the Jewish converts of Spain and Portugal who, forbidden from professing Judaism, were forced to practice it secretly which generated the phenomenon of *marranism*.[24] Those stereotyped representations of the Jews would cross centuries and join forces with the figure of the Jewish conspirator propagated by the *Protocols of the Elders of Zion* in the nineteenth and twentieth centuries.[25]

Artistic representations such as the traditional paintings of the Holy Communion, the kiss of Judas and the drama of the Passion (found in the pictures of the Stations of the Cross and in popular open-air representations) continued to incite hatred against Jews. The image of Judas was, over the centuries, transformed into the legendary figure of the "traitor", the villain or someone of unfaithful conduct. Although Jesus and all his disciples were Jews, in the preparatory studies produced by Leonardo da Vinci for *The Last Supper*, Judas is the only one who is distinguished by exaggerated traits, identified by his yellow garments that were mandatory for Jews in some European countries. According to the Gospels, after supper Jesus went to pray with the apostles at the Gethsemane Garden. It was there that Judas, in exchange for thirty gold coins, identified Christ to the guards by giving him a kiss and calling him a master. According to Matthew (27:3–10), Judas repented, returned the money and immediately hanged himself.

---

24 Maria Luiza Tucci Carneiro, *Preconceito Racial em Portugal e Brasil Colônia*, 3rd ed., São Paulo, Perspectiva, 2004.

25 Pierre-André Taguieff, *Les Protocoles des Sages de Sion*, vol. 1. *Introduction à l'Étude des Protocoles: un faux et ses usages dans le siècle*, Paris, Berg International, 1992.

4. Leonardo da Vinci. *The Last Supper*, 460 × 880 cm, 1498. Mixed technique with predominance of tempera and oil on two layers of plaster preparation applied to the plaster (stucco). Refectory of the Convent of Santa Maria delle Grazie, Milan, Italy. https://www.haltadefinizione.com/en/image-bank/. Access: 10.08.2019

5. Giotto. *The Kiss of Judas*, fresco, 200 × 185 cm, 1304–1306, no. 31. Scenes from the life of Christ. Capella degli Scrovegni, Padua, Italy. https://pt.wikipedia.org/wiki/Cappella_egli_Scrovegni#/media/Ficheiro:Giotto_-_Scrovegni_-_-31-_-_Kiss_of_Judas.jpg. Access"08.09.2019.

This scene became one of the icons of sacred painting, and contributed to affirm the image of the Jews as traitors. I refer here to an anonymous painting from the 12th century entitled *The Kiss of Judas,* whose theme reappears in the fresco painted by Giotto between 1304 and 1306 in the Scrovegni Chapel in Padua, Italy. It is also present in the fresco *The Last Supper,* produced between 1495 and 1498 by Leonardo da Vinci in the Church of *Santa Maria delle Grazie,* in Milan. Based on the passage of the New Testament (John 13:21), in which Jesus announces to the twelve apostles that among them one would betray him, Da Vinci highlights the figure of Judas at the *Pessach* table. There are also: *The Taking of Christ,* by Caravaggio or one of his disciples, painted in 1602; *The Kiss of Judas,* by Fra Angelico, from 1450, in Florence; The Apollinaris of Ravenna, from the 6th century; the famous *The Kiss of Judas,* by Jean Bourdichon, *c.* 1505, which is part of the manuscript *The Great Hours of Anna of Brittany*; Simão Rodrigues' *Kiss of Judas,* which is under the custody of the Leiria Museum (Portugal).

In the Gospel according to John (12:6 and 13:29) – the fourth and last in the Bible to be written between 95 and 100 – Judas, as the treasurer of the group of disciples, carries a moneybag; he also steals coins from the common fund. Both the moneybag and the coins are, still today, constant elements in antisemitic cartoons.[26] Not even Dante Alighieri (1265–1321), in the *Divine Comedy,* forgot the Jews or Judas who, in the depths of hell, was placed beside Cassius and Brutus, murderers of Julius Caesar. There, the three greatest traitors in history are then devoured by Lucifer. But it is worth to reproduce here a section of the Divine Comedy:

---

26 Vamberto Morais, *Pequena História do Anti-semitismo,* São Paulo, Difel, 1972, pp. 132–133.

6. Jean Bourdichon, *Le Baiser de Judas*, c. 1505, part of *Les Grandes Heures d'Anne de Bretagne*. National Library of France. http://autourdemesromans.com/wp-content/uploads/2015/02/Grandes-Heures-d-Anne-de-Bretagne-Latin-9474-227v.jpg. Access: 08.09.2019.

7. Simão Rodrigues, *The Kiss of Judas*, 1605–1607, oil on canvas, 57.5 × 82.0 cm, Episcopal Palace of Leiria. Leiria Museum, Portugal.

Ne'er then was penalty so just as that
Inflicted by the Cross, if thou regard
The nature in assumption doom'd; ne'er wrong
So great, in reference to Him, who took
Such nature on Him, and endured the doom.
So different effects flow'd from one act:
For by one death God and the Jews were pleased;
And Heaven was open'd, though the earth did
quake.[27]

The image of the traitorous Jew was intensely publicized in Nazi Germany by the newspaper *Der Stürmer,* which in August 1936 published a caricature depicting the Jew as a traitor. The headline read: "Betrayal / Schmulewitz's Judgment in Magdeburg / Stürmer Special Edition"; while the caption explained: "The book of Jude / The Devil himself wrote the Talmud with the blood and tears of non-Jews."

The Judas Puppet

The intensity of this myth, which is one of the main sources of medieval and modern antisemitism, left deep traces in the Christian imagination. Even today, children educated in Catholicism have their childhood marked by the figure of Judas, the man who "sold" and betrayed Jesus Christ. So much so that

27 According to the translator's remarks: "The death of Christ was pleasing to God, inasmuch as it satisfied the divine justice; and to the Jews, because it gratified their malignity; and while Heaven opened for joy at man's ransom, the earth trembled through compassion for its Maker." Dante Alighieri, *The Divine Comedy. Paradise. Canto VII.* Harvard Classics, 1909–1914, http://www.bartleby.com/20/307.html. Retrieved: May 22, 2018.

Der Stürmer

Deutsches Wochenblatt zum Kampfe um die Wahrheit

HERAUSGEBER: JULIUS STREICHER

Nummer 34 | Nürnberg, im August 1936 | 14. Jahr 1936

Staatsbetrug

Der Schmulewitzprozeß in Magdeburg

Sonderbericht des Stürmers

Die Olympischen Spiele des Jahres 1936 sind zu Ende gegangen. Dennoch weilen noch Tausende ausländischer Gäste bei uns. Sie wollen das Neue Deutschland kennen lernen. Sie wollen die Wahrheit erfahren über jenes Land, über das die Weltpresse seit Jahren die widersprechendsten Meldungen bringt. Vor allem ist es die Judenpresse, die immer und immer wieder über „Justizmorde" im Neuen Deutschland berichtet. Von den [illegible] Verbrechen der [illegible]rassigen Gauner schweigt sie natürlich kein Wort.

Die Olympiagäste haben Gelegenheit in unserer heutigen Stürmerausgabe einen typischen Fall jüdischer Devisenverbrechen kennenzulernen. Sie werden daraus ersehen, wie sich das deutsche Volk auch heute noch jüdischer Volksausbeuter zu erwehren hat. Mögen sie nach ihrer Rückkehr in die Heimat prüfen, ob es nicht auch in ihrem Vaterlande eine Judenfrage gibt.

Vor einem Jahre fand in der alten Elbestadt Magdeburg der Prozeß gegen den jüdischen Rassenschänder Albert Hirschland statt. Der Jude hatte in seiner Eigenschaft als Direktor einer Magdeburger Handelsschule Hunderte von jungen deutschen Mädchen geschändet und an Leib und Seele verdorben. Ein eigenartiger Zufall will es, daß die Stadt Magdeburg nun wieder der Schauplatz eines sensationellen Judenprozesses geworden ist. Der Inhaber des Magdeburger Judenbankhauses Philipp Schmulewitz und seine Rassegenossen Jenny Lederer, Max und Ilse Friedländer hatten sich vor der Großen Strafkammer Magdeburg wegen großer Devisenschiebungen zu verantworten.

Wer die Zeitung aufmerksam verfolgt, wird nahezu alltäglich von neuen jüdischen Devisenschiebungen lesen. Und er wird fragen: „Wie kommt es, daß gerade die Juden immer und immer wieder Devisenverbrechen begehen?" Wer die Judenfrage kennt und vor allem die Anweisungen kennt, die im jüdischen Geheimgesetzbuch Talmud niedergelegt sind, wird sich darüber nicht wundern. Hier steht geschrieben:

„Es ist erlaubt die nichtjüdische Obrigkeit um den Zoll zu betrügen. Es ist erlaubt zu schmuggeln. Denn

Aus dem Inhalt

Lloyd Georges Enthüllungen
Der Sieg der Anständigkeit
Die Talmudguillotine
Kleine Nachrichten aus aller Welt
Ein Talmudtriumph

Die Bücher Judas

Der Teufel selbst hat sie mit dem Blut und den Tränen der Nichtjuden geschrieben

Die Juden sind unser Unglück!

8. Fips, pseudonym of Philipp Rupprecht. Antisemitic caricature published by the newspaper *Der Stürmer* with the image of the "traitor Jew". Nuremberg, Bavaria, Germany, August 14, 1936. United States Holocaust Memorial Museum, courtesy of Helen Fagin, ID: Collections: 1990.89.1. Available at: https://collections.ushmm.org/search/catalog/pa1093181. Access: 10.08.2019.

a collective acceptance persists in several European and Ibero-American countries about the symbolic meaning of burning Judas Iscariot for his betrayal of Christ, on the Holy Saturday of Glory. The massacre of Judas usually takes place on Easter Saturday, that is, during the Holy Week, with local variations. In recent decades it has been common to use the figure of Judas for political criticism, using posters hanging from the neck and even replacing his face with the countenance of some corrupt politician. Passed down from generation to generation, the rite should not be interpreted as a folkloric phenomenon, but as an example of cultural transfiguration and expression of traditional antisemitism. Here we found ourselves before the survival of a pagan feast (Roman Compitals) called by the Catholic Church "The Burning of Judas", which was later adapted to the purpose of symbolically burning a puppet representing Judas, the Jew who betrayed Christ.

According to Ático Vilas-Boas da Mota, a scholar devoted to the study of this rite in Brazilian folklore, the burning of Judas is the "survival of the condemnation in effigy"; it is a formula sustained by the Iberian Inquisition to condemn those who managed to escape or who died before being sentenced. Although it is a "transfigured folklore residue", the lynching of Judas translates persecutions into the purging practices that occurred throughout the Middle Ages. In other words, this rite of purging is intended to eliminate everything that symbolizes evil and, as such, being instrumental to the unbalance of the established order.[28]

At the end of the 19th century, for example, this ritual was observed in Corsica, in Lizing (German Lorraine), in Nelling and Mittelbronn. Similar customs were found in other parts of Europe: Tyrol, Upper Bavaria, Franconia, Cologne, Saarland, England, Switzerland, Portugal, Spain etc., and in Latin America, in countries such as Brazil, Chile, Peru, Uruguay and Venezuela.

In the Upper Rhine, "the burning of Judas" symbolized "the burning of the Jew, the red Jew or the eternal Jew. In Portugal, while the Judas burned, light bulbs exploded throughout the puppet's body, possibly inspired by inquisitorial practices".[29]

This pantomime of extraordinary theatrical effect – a kind of Roman circus with different protagonists – goes beyond the spectacle of commemoration, and assumes characteristics typical of popular antisemitism: from paranoia to collective hysteria. As participants in this ritual, adults and children often justify their aggressiveness against the figure of the "traitor Judas Iscariot" because "he is bad", "he killed our Father in heaven", "because it is a revenge of Catholics against Jews", "because he sold Jesus and condemned him to Calvary".

In Spain, for example, the Feast of Judas still follows the Catholic tradition and takes place in several villages such as: Robledo de Chavela (Madrid), Pedro Abad (Cordoba), Venta del Moro (Valencia), Villadiego (Burgos), Chozas de Canales (Toledo), Talayuelas (Cuenca), Cabezuela del Valle (Caceres), Samaniego (Álava), among others. According to the historian Javier Domínguez Arribas, the themes of deicide, ritual crimes and sacrileges – considered as "traces of traditional anti-

28 Ático Vilas-Boas da Mota, *Queimação de Judas: Catarismo, Inquisição e Judeus no Folclore Brasileiro*, Rio de Janeiro, MEC; SEAC; Funarte; Instituto Nacional do Folclore, 1981.

29 Rossini Tavares de Lima, *Folclore das Festas Cíclicas*, Rio de Janeiro, Irmãos Vitale Editores, 1971, pp. 37–59. Descriptions of those rituals can be found in Jean Baptiste Debret, *Viagem Pitoresca e Histórica ao Brasil*, São Paulo, Livraria Martins Fontes, 1940; Euclides da Cunha, *À Margem da História*, 5. ed., Porto, Lello & Irmãos, 1941 (1 ed. 1909); Gustavo Barroso, *Coração de Menino*, Rio de Janeiro, Getúlio M. Costa Editor, 1939; Oswaldo Rocha Lima, *Pedaços do Sertão*, Rio de Janeiro, A. Coelho Branco Filho Editor, 1940.

9. V. T. "Judas", President of the Province of Pernambuco, 26.0 × 38.0 cm. *América Illustrada, Jornal Humorístico*, Typographia Americana, Recife, July 13, 1879, Year IX, n. 27, p. 4. Newspaper Library, Public Archive of Pernambuco/PE.

Judaism" – (re)appear in several local celebrations in Spain, especially during the Holy Week. As examples, Domínguez Arribas alludes to the custom of "killing Jews" in Sahagún and other Leonese localities, and of consuming a kind of *sangria* wine in Catalonia and Asturias.

In Brazil and especially in the State of São Paulo the *Autos da Malhação de Judas* (*Autos* of the Lynching of Judas) that take place in cities such as Itú, Cotia, Capivari and Pirapora do Bom Jesus, are well known. In April 1849, the newspaper *O Campineiro* registered news about the stoning of a Judas made of straw and some of the verses uttered by the participants:

1. Judeu, Judeu / O Português / Que apanhou do espanhol!

2. Judas foi para Roma / Vender Jesus / Depois foi enforcado / O coitado[30]

The image of the treacherous Judas appears once again published, on June 13th, 1879, by a newspaper from Pernambuco State called *América Illustrada*. In it we can see a caricature created by V. T., in which Adolpho de Barros Cavalcanti Lacerda, president of the Province of Pernambuco, is criticized as a two-faced man: a traitor or an angel. As a traitor, Adolpho Lacerda is presented by Judas who, without any feature that identifies him as a Jew, carries the traditional bag of money in one hand and kisses a woman who, symbolically, represents the Liberal Party. The closing of the Provincial Assembly during Lacerda's administration was criticized here as a betrayal to the Liberal Party, which he led.[31]

A New Dress for an Old Hatred

"A new dress for an old hatred" is a definition that Pilar Rahola uses in one of her articles in which she discusses the strength of myths and the resurgence of antisemitism today. Here in this breviary, I follow her reasoning and argumentation. Jews continue to be held responsible for the death of Jesus Christ as

30 1. Jew, Jew / The Portuguese / Who was beaten by the Spaniard!

2. Judas went to Rome / To sell Jesus / He was hanged afterwards / The poor thing! "Ao Público" [To the public], in *O Campineiro*, April 10th, 1849, São Paulo, Typografia Liberal, 1849, pp. 13–14. Biblioteca J. Mindlin/USP-SP.

31 The sisters Maria das Graças and Rosário Ataíde have carried out an important iconographic research that was published in *História (nem sempre) bem-humorada de Pernambuco*, vol. 1, Recife, Edições Bagaço, 1999, p. 133.

if they were reptiles or Satan. That subject has never left the agenda, even after *Nostra Aetate,* declared by the Ecumenical Council of Vatican II. On the contrary, it continues to be updated by conservative Catholic currents and anti-Israel movements. It suffices to take a look at some Arab newspapers, for example, to see that Western antisemitic myths can be found both in print and between the lines. It is common to find in those newspapers – among them the *Al-Istiqal* – that the Jews killed Christ (or that they murdered Palestinians), as well as references reproduced from *The Protocols of the Elders of Zion,* which is available in Arabic since 1927. The same tone is held in newspapers that represent the French Muslim world, which, through caricatures, update the antisemitic myths, including the "deicide" one, which is triggered to explain the Israel/Palestine conflict. As an example, in September 2012, during a whole week, about ten antisemitic cartoons were published in important Muslim newspapers in France, including the *Al-Bayan, Ad-Dustour, Al-Raya* and *Al-Watan.* By retaking the matrices of Nazi cartoons, the caricaturists demonize and animalize the Jews.[32]

Menachem Milson, a professor of Arabic language and literature at the Hebrew University of Jerusalem who analyzed those libels states:

> Blood libels are still commonplace in the Arab and Muslim world. They still flourish in major official newspapers. Some authors recycle and reactivate those accusations,

32 Caricatures reproduced in the article "Cette semaine, au moins 10 caricatures offensantes pour les juifs dans les médias musulmans", in JSS News, September 24th, 2015. Available at: http://jssnews.com/2012/09/24/caricarabes

adding new distortions. For example, that Jews use human blood not only for the preparation of *matzah* (bread unleavened) but also as a filling for *humantaschen*, a puffy dough for the feast of Purin, according to a Saudi newspaper.[33]

Cinema has also revived the myth that the Jewish people are deicidal: I refer here to the controversial film *The Passion of Christ*, directed by Mel Gibson and released in the Holy Week 2004. The fact that this film was praised by some Vatican authorities convinced a larger audience of how serious the approach taken by its director was. Contradicting the myth, Evangelist Billy Graham considered the script as "faithful to the biblical teachings that claim that we are all responsible for the death of Jesus, because we all sin. But it was our sins that caused His death, not any particular group".[34] However, his considerations did not echo. A blockbuster in the United States and other countries, the film revived that judeophobic myth by bringing to the fore the traditional question: "Who killed Christ?". New masks for a secular myth or, as Pilar Rahola very well defined it, "a new dress for an old hatred":

> Just as it is impossible to completely explain the historical evil of anti-Semitism, it is also not possible to totally explain the present-day imbecility of anti-Israelism. Both drink from the fountain of intolerance and lies. Also, if we accept that anti-Israelism is the new form of anti-Semitism,

---

33 Arno Froese, "A Mais Perigosa Forma de Ódio aos Judeus – Os Árabes Adotam Mitos Anti-semitas Europeus", *Notícias de Israel*, August, 2013.

34 Billy Graham, [Reverend], "Billy Graham Screens 'The Passion of the Christ'". In: *WND*, Nov. 26th, 2003, http://www.wnd.com/2003/11/22003/

> we conclude that circumstances may have changed, but the deepest myths, both of the Medieval Christian anti-Semitism and of the modern political anti-Semitism, are still intact. Those myths are part of the chronicle of Israel. For example, the Medieval Jew accused of killing Christian children to drink their blood connects directly with the Israeli Jew who kills Palestinian children to steal their land. Always they are innocent children and dark Jews.[35]

We consider that the concept of deicide remains today with two historical occurrences as watershed moments: the death of Jesus Christ and the declaration *Nostra Aetate* (In Our Time), published during the Second Vatican Council. Although the Catholic Church has excluded the definition of deicide, it is still important to consider that, centuries ago, the Catholic doctrine revealed in the New Testament that the Jewish authorities had accused Jesus of blasphemy and promoted his execution using the authority of Pontius Pilate, governor of the Province of Judea. And while historians and theologians may argue about the veracity of those historical facts, such accusations have brought grave consequences to the Jewish people. Exactly because this is a historical dilemma, we must not allow doubts to further proliferate by instigating acts of intolerance.

Aware of the danger of the antisemitic discourse, the Catholic Church has revised its positions since the Second Vatican Council when, in October 1965, the *Nostra Aetate* declaration was published and suppressed the Catholic accusation against the Jewish people. By implicitly acknowl-

---

35 Pilar Rahola, *Jews With Six Arms*. Available in English at: http://www.aish.com/jw/s/96560674.html. Retrieved: Feb. 19, 2019.

edging its past faults, the Vatican gives us the image that, from then onwards, a new mentality would settle in the Catholic world, unanimously. In the case of the deicide myth, the roots are ancient and calcified by dogmas. This statement explains the tension and controversy generated by the *Nostra Aetate* declaration, today a watershed moment in Christian thought about Judaism. For historian John Connelly – author of *From Enemy to Brother: The Revolution in Catholic Teaching on the Jews* – those large changes were articulated by Jewish-born clergymen who forced the reforms at the Second Vatican Council.[36]

In short, to some opponents of those new trends in Catholic theology, they were "worthy of an antipope", and disclosed the actions of Jews who were "trying to alter the order of things", that is, "the Antichrist was present in Rome" and the Papacy was being "manipulated by forces averse to Christian truth". Numerous Catholic movements – as expected – interpreted *Nostra Aetate* as an apostasy, a moment of crisis that would lead the Catholic faith towards agony. More conservative cardinals formed an opposition front trying to annul the statement which – in addition to condemning all forms of hatred, including antisemitism – claimed that Jesus, his mother Mary and the apostles were Jewish and that the Church was originated in the Old Testament. Voices of resistance to change compared that moment with the "passage from the darkness at a time eclipses to the collapse of a Catholic demolition in the space of five decades". Numerous Catholic magazines rejected this policy of ecumenical opening, including the French

36 John Connelly, "Converts who Changed the Church". In: *Forward*, July 30, 2012. http://forward.com/opinion/159955/converts-who-changed-the-church/. Retrieved: May 31, 2018.

Itinéraires, Nouvelles de Chrétienté, Verbe and *Action Fatima-la-Salette.*[37]

In 2005, forty years after the declaration *Nostra Aetate* by the Second Vatican Council, Pope John Paul II received in the Vatican 160 rabbis and liturgical singers from Israel, the United States and Europe, thus strengthening the Catholic–Jewish dialogue. Today there is great expectation about the reconciliation of the Catholic Church with its own past and the Jews, now passed on to the current Pope Francis I, a former archbishop of Buenos Aires, elected on March 13th, 2013. The wound remains open even though Francis has acknowledged that *Nostra Aetate* is a reference in the relations with the Jewish people.[38]

37 Ariel Danielle, "Nada de Novo: É o Próprio Bergoglio a Confirmar-se Herege", in *Pro.Roma. Mariana,* December 30, 2013. http://promariana.wordpress.com/2013/12/30/nada-de-novo-e-o-proprio-bergoglio-a-confirmar-se-herege/ . Retrieved: May 31, 2018.

38 Peter E. Gordon, "The Border Crossers", in *New Republic,* May 18, 2012; http://www.newrepublic.com/article/books-and-arts/magazine/103331/catholic-jewish-anti-semitism-pope-vatican-nazis . Retrieved May 31, 2018.

MYTH 2

The Jews Are a Secret Entity

The myth says that the Jews are a secret entity that "conspires to control the world". Indeed, those rumors, like many others about Jews, continue to get through the deepest strata of Western culture, sustaining a rancidity inherited from traditional antisemitism of a theological basis.

In the 21st century, that fear has been revitalized under the guise of a nuclear war allegedly orchestrated by the State of Israel and the angst about the end of the world, a feeling that has always dominated popular consciousness. This narrative, however, is rooted in the medieval hatred against Jews who, at various times, have been accused of acting in the shadows or in the underworld of societies, promoting plots, attacks, satanic rituals or black magic, conspiring against Christianity and instigating the slaughter of Christians. That is the part of the myth that lies, although, in this particular case, it holds some truth: between the 15th and 19th centuries, Jews actually practiced Judaism secretly, but not as a satanic sect or with the aim of conspiring to dominate the world or destroy Christianity.

Initially, the motives for such accusations were socio-political and relied on religious arguments that allowed the expropriation of property that belonged to new Christians, stigmatized as "impure" members of an "infected race". During the Inquisition, both in Portugal and Spain, this group was accused of practicing secret snoga (synagogue) in order to strengthen itself as a group and weaken the dogmas of the Catholic Church. Actually, new Christians, in order to escape the inquisitorial persecutions and the death penalty at the stake, had no choice but to plunge into *marranism*, that is, to secretly "Judaize" themselves in order to uphold the principles of Judaism, their religious practices and even to survive as a minority.

Especially from the 15th century onwards, the term *marrano* (which means pork, pig, according to the old Spanish vocabulary) was applied to define Jews and Moors who converted to Christianity. Bearing a derogatory sense, the word was associated with the idea of falsehood, untrustworthy, conspiracy and an infected race. According to Raphael Bluteau's dictionary published in 1713, "infecto de sangue chamamos a quem descende de Pays mouros ou de Judeos. Porque he herdado como infecto de sangue".[39] This definition refers to another entry that explains the meaning of being "pure-blooded" as opposed to "infected": "diz se hü christão-velho, sem casta de mouro, nem judeo. Pure sanguine genitus."[40] The concepts of purity and impurity of blood persisted throughout the 18th and 19th centuries and also encompassed blacks, mulattoes and gypsies. In the 20th century, in Nazi

39 "Of infected with blood are those who descend from Moore or Jewish parents. Because they have inherited a blood-borne infection". In, Raphael Bluteau, *Vocabulário Português e Latino, autorizado com exemplo dos melhores escritores portugueses e latinos e offerecido a El Rey de Portugal D. João V*, Coimbra, no Real Collegio das Artes e Cia de Jesus, MDCCXIII, pp. 122–134; Dicionário Exegético, por hum Anônymo, Lisboa, Officina Patriarcal de Franc. Ameno, 1781; Mario Fiuza, *Elucidário das Palavras, Termos e Frases, edição crítica baseada nos manuscritos e originais de Viterbo*. 1st ed., Lisboa, Livr. Civiliz, 1798/1799

40 "It is said of an Old Christian, neither More or Jew. A pure blood." *Ibidem.*

Germany, the expression "pure blood" was taken up to describe those who were of Aryan blood, thus proving the "purity of race".

Anita Novinsky, a pioneer in inquisitorial studies in Brazil, affirms that *marranism* must be interpreted as a resistance movement against the "imposition of a culture, symbolizing progress against stagnation, modernity against conservatism. As dissidents of the Christian order made up of the Catholic Church from the 15th century onwards, new Christians or *Marranos* were persecuted as heretics and treated as social outcasts. With the intention of escaping inquisitorial persecutions and death at the stake, the new Christians created forms of underground communication. It was in this context that the project to unify the kingdoms of Portugal and Spain – a country that, by tradition, denied the rights to "be different" to non-Catholic minorities – grew stronger.[41] One of the explanations that I share here, and was put forward by a stream of historians, is that old Christians were interested in preventing the advance of the commercial bourgeoisie (largely composed of elements of Jewish origin, usually successful traders) and thus preserving their privileges as representatives of a "pure race".[42]

41 Anita Novinsky, "Consideraciones sobre los Criptojudíos Hispano-Portugueses: El Caso de Brasil", in Ángel Alcala (org.), *Judíos, Sefarditas, Conversos. La Expulsión de 1492 y Sus Consecuencias*, New York/Madrid, Ed. Ámbito, 1992, pp. 513–522; "Marranes: Le judaisme laïque dans le nouveaux monde", in I. Roseman (org.), *Juifs laïques du Réligieux Vers le Culturel*, Paris, Corlet, 1992, pp. 92–96; Lina Gorenstein; Maria Luiza Tucci Carneiro (orgs.), *Ensaios sobre a Intolerância, Inquisição, Marranismo e Anti-semitismo*, São Paulo, Humanitas; Fapesp, 2002; Cecil Roth, *A History of the Marranos*, New York, Meridian Books; The Jewish Publication Society of America, 1959.

42 Antonio José Saraiva, *Inquisição e Cristãos-novos*, Porto, Inova, 1969; Anita Novinsky, *Cristãos-novos na Bahia*, São Paulo, Perspectiva, 1972.

Traces of the myth from the 15th to the 20th centuries can be found in several countries, in both Europe and the Americas. The fact that Judaism was banned during the modern era favored the process of secularization and integration of new Christians to the European society, where, from the 18th century, some had started to join Freemasonry. As representatives of an educated people (People of the Book) and adherents to the ideals of freedom, fraternity and equality, the Jews identified themselves with the principles of Freemasonry, which defends the idea of a society that values the free man, with no distinction of race, religion, political ideology or social position. Moreover, because many of the ethical principles, rites and symbols of Freemasonry emerged inspired by Judaism and the Old Testament. Once again, the belief that "Jews form a secret society" was nourished by a reality that, distorted by the "creators of myths", continued to instigate hatred against Jews.

Substantive antisemitic literature was disseminated in France and replicated itself in several European countries – such as Spain and Germany – and also in Latin America in countries such as Argentina and Brazil. Among the main authors who signed this bibliography-matrix were León de Poncins, Oscar de Férenzy, I. Bertrand, León Bloy and … Èdouard Drumont. The theories of French journalist and writer Leon de Poncins (1897–1976) reaffirmed the idea that Freemasonry was intimately related to Judaism and intended to unify the world under Jewish law.[43] Poncins was one of the main disseminators of the

43 Among works by León de Poncins see: *Sociétés des Nations Super-état Maçonique*, Paris, Gabriel Beauchesne et as fils, MCMXXXVI; *As Forças Secretas da Revolução: Maçonaria-Judaísmo*, Porto Alegre, Livraria do Globo, 1931. León de Poncins, *Freemasonry and the Vatican: A Struggle for Recognition*, Publisher Britons Publishing, 1968, p. 76.

thesis that Jews formed secret societies in alliance with the Freemasons, using a strong anti-Jewish, anti-communist and anti-progressive discourse. He devoted himself to denounce the hidden forces that corrupted Christianity, and influenced several intellectuals, including Brazilian theorist and integralist[44] Gustavo Barroso (1888–1959), who usually defended Poncins' theories. Leon de Poncins' work is part of a French matrix that, since the late 19th century, contributed to spread antisemitic thought modeled by political myths.[45]

44 The Brazilian Integralist movement was founded by Plínio Salgado, a journalist and a renowned writer who belonged to the modernist green-yellow current. After interviewing Benito Mussolini during a trip to Italy in 1930, he created the newspaper *A Razão* in São Paulo, whose editorials are expressive of nationalist and anti-liberal political conceptions. In February 1932, along with regional groups whose members were sympathetic to fascism and Catholic intellectuals of authoritarian tendencies, he created the *Sociedade de Estudos Políticos* [Political Studies Society] (SEP) and in October of that same year, the Brazilian Integralist Action (AIB), a political organization inspired by Italian fascism, whose ideas were expressed in the Integralist Manifesto. Their ideology was based on nationalism and corporatism aimed at a cultural revolution. The AIB maintained a hierarchical structure, with Plínio Salgado as its national leader, and was shaped by the cult of symbols and rituals inspired by European fascism. The group used the Greek letter sigma as an emblem. The militants, mobilized by the motto "God, Fatherland and Family", also performed a particular salute called the Anauê. Integralism became the largest mass movement with a fascist profile until 1938 when, after a failed coup attempt to overthrow Getúlio Vargas from power, Plínio Salgado was exiled in Portugal. In 1945, with the re-democratization, Plínio returned to Brazil and founded the Partido da Representação Popular [Popular Representation Party] (PRP).

45 I. Bertrand, *La Franc-Maçonnerie Sect Juive*, Paris, Blond, 1903; León Bloy, *Le Salut par les Juifs*, Paris, Librairie Adrien Dersay, 1892; Édouard Drumont, *La France Juive*, Paris, Flammarion Éditeur, 1938 (I. ed. 1912); Édouard Drummond, *Le Testament d'un Antisémite*, Paris, E. Dentu Éditeur, 1891.

Important studies on the myths of demon-populated secret societies were developed by historians. Among those writings are: *The Mythology of Secret Societies*, by John Roberts, *The Age of the Irrational*, by James Webb, *The Pursuit of the Millennium*, by Norman Cohn, *El Enemigo Judeo-masónico en la Propaganda Franquista (1936–1945)*, by Javier Domínguez Arribas.[46] Roberts believes that the rationalism of the Enlightenment and the Industrial Revolution led certain groups to believe that they "could dominate or control the reality". James Webb, in turn, calls attention to the atmosphere of anxiety and uncertainty that, during the 19th century, allowed the proliferation of superstition at a moment when individuals found out that they were the "arbiters of their own destiny". Norman Cohn, a pioneer and theoretician of this new historiography, puts his finger on a real sore spot by stating that the medieval millennium that subsidized the slaughter of thousands of Jews had common features with modern genocidal movements. Cohn innovated in his 1967 book *Warrant for Genocide* by associating the theme of anti-Judaism and anti-Satanism to the myth of the conspiracy of the *Elders of Zion* and the genocidal delusions of the Nazis.[47]

Historian Javier Domínguez Arribas in his study *El Enemigo Judeo-masónico en la Propaganda Franquista* [The Jewish-Masonic

46 John Roberts, *Mythology of Secret Societies*, London, Secker & Warburg, 1972; James Webb, *The Age of the Irrational: The Flight from Reason*, London, Macdonald & Co., 1971, vol. I; *The Occult Establishment*, Open Court La Salle, 1976, vol. II; Norman Cohn, *The Pursuit of the Millenium: Revolutionary Millenarians and Mystical Anarchists of the Middle Ages*, London and New York, Oxford University Press, 1970; León Poliakov, *A Causalidade Diabólica 1. Ensaio sobre a Origem das Perseguições*, translation Alice Kyoko Miyashiro, São Paulo, Perspectiva; Associação Universitária de Cultura Judaica, 1991; Javier Dominguez Arribas, *op. cit.*

47 Norman Cohn, *op. cit.*

Enemy in Franco's Propaganda], an analysis of anti-semitism and anti-freemasonry during Francoism, also introduces new ideas, based on an unpublished documentary *corpus* selected to explain the origins, proliferation and functions of the Jewish-Masonic myth in Spain. Arribas distinguishes between visible (in this case communists) and invisible (Jews and Freemasons) enemies, reinforcing the idea that the myth does not need actual physical existence of an adversary of the Nation and/or its people. The author states that "speeches about Jews and Freemasons spread by the Francoist propaganda had no relation to reality".[48] In addition, from the forced expulsion of Jews by the Catholic Monarchs in 1492 and the virulent actions of the Inquisition against New Christians, Spain had remained "free of Jews", an expression based on the myth of the purity of blood that proliferated in Spain after the promulgation of the Toledo Statutes (1449).

Analyzing the logic of mistrust that moved Franco's propaganda, Arribas reveals the paths traveled by the Jewish-masonic myth through a discourse disseminated in newspapers, pamphlets, (combat) literature, school books and syllabi presented by the regime's "official (or unofficial) propaganda that emanated from the center of Franco's power". The author also mentions the role played by catechisms and pastoral letters written by Catholic bishops, filled with antisemitic and anti-freemasonry instruments of persuasion that were used to mobilize the conservative masses. Finally, the Spanish historiography proves that, due to the absence of Jews in Francoist Spain, anti-semitism was much more a subject linked to propaganda, with no consequences in terms of persecution and extermination of the group.[49]

48 *Ibidem*, p. 23.

49 *Ibidem*, p. 16

Javier Arribas indicates as a reference date for the birth of anti-freemasonry, the year 1698 when a pamphlet printed in a flyer format (11 × 16 cm) circulated in London warning Christians against "this diabolical sect" because of its secret character and its connections with the Antichrist. In Scotland, a letter dated from 1690–1691, in which Pastor Robert Kirk associated the word Freemason to the rabbinical tradition, circulated in the country; in Spain, the first reference to the founders of Freemasonry with an accusing tone came from the inquisitor Valladolid Andrés Ignacio Orbe who, in 1745, wrote that "its founders, I am afraid, had something of Judaism". But, according to Domínguez Arribas, it was in the letter sent by the Piedmontese captain Jean-Baptiste Simonini to Abbot Barruel in 1806 that the Jewish-Masónic myth emerged as an alert. Simonini criticizes Barruel for not having mentioned in his Memoirs the responsibility of the "Jewish sect" among the lot of "infernal sects that are opening the way to the Antichrist".[50]

Appealing to the trilogy Judaism, Freemasonry and Satanism, Pope Pius IX defined Freemasonry as the "Synagogue of Satan", an expression applied in the encyclical *Etsi multa*. Those accusations were replicated in France and Spain through publications that, in their titles and contents, announced the secrets of the Jewish–Masonic–Satanic plot. In the 20th century, with the proliferation of the *Protocols of the Elders of Zion* in Europe and America, the myth of the Judeo-Masonic covenant was renewed. In Spain, several editions of the *Protocols* devoted to the "Judeo-Masónic dangers" were published in 1920, 1922, 1927 and 1932, always enriched with complementary notes. Their 1932 edition received critical comments from M. E. Jouin

50 An extensive inventory of anti-Masonic and antisemitic works written in Spain in the 18th and 19th centuries can be found in the chapter "La genealogía del enemigo judeo-masónico", by Javier Dominguez Arribas, *op. cit.*, pp. 51–66; 363–401.

– a publisher, editor of the preface, an Apostolic Protonotary and Priest of St. Augustine – who announced, "the world domination of Israel, represented by the symbolic serpent".[51]

The accusation that the "Jews act as a secret society" echoed in the first version of the apocryphal book *The Protocols of the Wise Ancient Scholars of Zion*, published by the St. Petersburg newspaper *Znamya* (The Flag), in the context of the political conflicts that marked Tsarist Russia between 1903 and 1917. A set of 24 lectures (1903–1905) demonstrated that the "erudite ancient Jews" organized themselves into a secret and multidimensional community, that sought to put into practice the "program for the conquest of the world by the Jews". Without any chronological boundaries, the texts offered a logical interpretation for chaos, universality and timelessness as being the main structural characteristics of this myth.

The idea of the Judeo-Masonic plot reappeared in Spain in 1935 in Francisco de Luis's *La Masonería contra España* [Masonry against Spain] considered by Arribas as one of the most important anti-Jewish-Masonic works of the 1930s. During the Spanish Civil War (1936–1939) demonstrations against Jews and Freemasons were carried out by Franco's supporters who, in addition to identifying themselves with the Nazi ideology, had works of French Catholicism as their matrices of thought. The Francoist press was entitled to invoke the Jewish–Masonic–Bolshevik plot in articles that warned about the infiltration of those enemies into national ranks and the International Brigades. Franco's obsession was to fight both Freemasonry and Communism which, in his opinion, conspired against the regen-

51 *Los Protocolos de los Sabios de Sion*. Edición completa y comentarios críticos de M. E. Jouin. Spanish translation by del Duque de la Victoria. Madrid, Ediciones FAX, 1932 (reedited in 2008).

eration of Spain. It was in this context that two pieces of legislation were promulgated: the Law of Political Responsibilities issued on 13 February 1939 and the Law for the Repression of Freemasonry and Communism in March 1940, which legitimized the persecution of the "enemies of the regime".[52]

The Judeo-Masonic discourse received some more visibility in 1941 after the creation of the Toledo Editions, a collection idealized by Fernandez Flórez, under the responsibility of the Editions and Publications Section of Franco's National Propaganda Delegation. The texts were dogmatic and based on highly persuasive iconographic elements that fulfilled the political function of the myth: an attack to rival factions, discrediting them before society. Some of the published booklets gained notoriety. For example, among others: *La Masonería en Acción* [Freemasonry in Action] (1941), by an anonymous author; *Cartas a un Cacique* [Letters to a Chieftain], by phalangist Bartolomé Soler (1942); *La Masonería Femenina* [The Female Freemasonry] (anonymous, 1942); *Camarada: He aquí el enemigo* [Comrade: Behold the enemy!], by Federico de Urrutia; *Andanzas del Bulo*, [Wanderings of the hoax], by Francisco Ferrari Billoch (1942); *La Garra del Capitalismo Judío* [The Claws of Jewish Capitalism] (anonymous, 1943).[53]

During the Nazi period, the fear of Jews would expand even further and include accusations against communists who, according to the regime ideologues, like the Jews, acted in the shadows and dark recesses of the society, conspiring against the German nation. World conspiracies (Jewish, Marxists, Freemasons etc.) were denounced by the National-Socialist authorities by means of movies, the press, iconographic exhibi-

52 Javier Domínguez Arribas, *op. cit.*, pp. 166, 201, 203.

53 Idem, *op. cit.*, pp. 363–408.

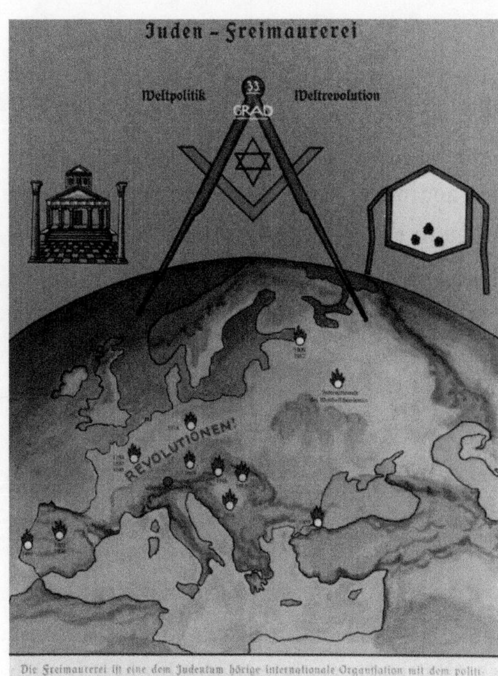

Juden - Freimaurerei
Weltpolitik
33
GRAD
Weltrevolution
REVOLUTIONEN!
Die Freimaurerei ist eine dem Judentum hörige internationale Organisation mit dem politischen Ziel, dem Judentum auf dem Wege der Weltrevolution die Herrschaft zu verschaffen!

10. Unidentified author. *Illustrated world map with masonic symbols*. Poster n. 64 of the series "Erbiehre und Rassenkunde" [Theory of Inheritance and Racial Hygiene]. Stuttgart, National Literature, c. 1935. PD-Art.

tions and official speeches. Hundreds of posters were created and distributed throughout Germany and the occupied countries, whose aim was inciting hatred against Jews based on a theory of an international Jewish-Masonic conspiracy. I refer here to a German poster of 1935 that displays in its title the duo "World Politics–World Revolution" mediated by Freemasonry which, allegedly dominated by the Jews, establishes political relations to achieve Jewish domination by means of a world revolution. The image displays the main symbols of Freemasonry: the temple, the square and compass, the apron, the hexagram (interlaced triangles), the number 33 representing the greatest degree occupied by the great master, who was the guardian and conductor of Freemasonry. In several countries, the "revolutionary outbursts" are marked with white and red symbols.

Another example of this accusatory logic is the panel created for the anti-Bolshevik exhibition in occupied France, which represents the alleged tendency of Judaism to world hegemony. Opened in Paris in March 1942, that exhibition expressed the German crusade against Judaism, Freemasonry and Bolshevism. The message in the title lies on the figure of a Jew identified by his aquiline nose, the Star of David sewn to his clothes, his curls and a *quipah*.

The argument is, once again, that Germany was defending itself from the international threat represented by the "world Jewry" that acted in the backstage of societies. That became a recurring theme for Nazi propaganda which, using such images, sought to summon the population of the occupied countries to "make a total war" [*Totaler Krieg*] against the Russians, as well as to incite hatred against the Jews. Prior to that event, the government had issued a set of antisemitic laws to speed up the "Aryanization" process, that is, to segregate the French Jewish population. Treated as outcasts, Jews were expelled from administrative and teaching positions, the liberal professions, the world of finance, theatre, movies, etc. The force of the myths against the Jews that had remained there for centuries favored the application of antisemitic laws such as the one promulgated on July 22nd, 1941, which included the confiscation of property, justified by the intention to "eliminate all Jewish influence on world economy" according to the provisions of the *Protocols*. Historian Michel Winock estimates that in the first years of the occupation "15,000 families or a total of at least 60,000 people lost their means of survival in the occupied zone".[54]

54 Michel Winock, *La France et les Juifs, de 1789 à nos Jours*, Paris, Éditions du Seuil, 2004, p. 226.

11. Unidentified author. Image that illustrates the cover of the booklet *La Masoneria en Acción*, one of the titles of the collection by Ediciones Toledo. Madrid, 1941, 71 pages. Tucci Collection/ State of São Paulo/Brazil.

12. "El Judaismo", illustration from the book *La Garra del Capitalismo Judío*, unidentified author. Madrid. Ediciones Toledo, 1943. National Library of Spain.

The trilogy Judaism–Masonry–Secret Sects instigated an antisemitic and anti-communist discourse in several countries, and attracted a number of followers. In Brazil, this gave ground to both racist and politically intolerant actions during Getúlio Vargas's administration in the 1930s and 1940s. Jackson de Figueiredo, for example, who was an extreme right-wing Catholic intellectual, had been warning, since the 1920s, of the menacing dangers of Protestantism and against the invasion by Masonry and International Judaism, considered as threatening

13a. Matrices of the myth published in Brazil: *A Maçonaria, Seita Judaica*, by I. Bertrand, translated by Gustavo Barroso (1938), Cover

13b. *Judaísmo, Maçonaria e Comunismo*, by Gustavo Barroso (1937), Cover. Tucci Collection/ State of São Paulo/Brazil.

menaces. The Brazilian Catholic thinker Alceu Amoroso Lima – who wrote under the pseudonym Trystão de Athayde – also warned against "the dangers of Judaism, Masonry, Spiritism, Communism and Protestantism".[55]

Even Oswaldo Aranha, the Brazilian ambassador to the United States at that time, suggested to Getúlio Vargas a

55 Magazine *A Ordem* (53), 4:5, cited by Celso da Cunha, *Educação e Autoritarismo no Estado Novo*, São Paulo, Cortez, 1981, p. 94. See also Enrique Luz, *"O Eterno Judeu": Anti-semitismo e Antibolchevismo nos Cartazes de Propaganda Política Nacional-Socialista (1939–1945)*, Masters Dissertation in History, School of Philosophy and Human Sciences, Federal University of Minas Gerais, 2006.

program of universal struggle against Freemasonry, Communism and Judaism. He argued that Brazil was dominated by liberal Freemasonry at the service of extremist ideas. He accused Judaism of creating and maintaining an "environment capable of dislocating this civilization to the abyss" and that if this tendency continued to be manipulated by the Jewish spirit, "it would drag this entire civilization into a new regime, similar to the Russian". This accusation does not differ much from the content propagated by I. Bertrand in his work *La Franc-maçonnerie Secte juive ses origines, son esprit et le but qu'elle poursuit* [Freemasonry, Jewish Sect: Its Origins, its spirit and its goals], translated into Portuguese by Gustavo Barroso in 1938, as well as *Judaísmo, Maçonaria e Comunismo* [Judaism, Freemasonry and Communism], by Gustavo Barroso, published in 1937.

Persistence of the Accusation

Under the bias of modern antisemitism, the persistent accusation is that the "conspiratorial Jews" are part of the "world Jewry" that dominates parliaments, the press, the economy, the media, education, etc., a discourse based on the accusations propagated by the *Protocols of the Elders of Zion*.

Versions such as those arose in response to the declaration *Nostra Aetate* (In Our Time) issued by the Vatican in October 1965, considered by its opponents as apostasy. The old accusatory speech that enemies (in this case, Jews and Freemasons) plotted against the Church for its scourge, since the "Masonic occupation of the Vatican", was, once again, put into circulation. The extent of the damage caused by the ecumenical opening was recorded in the book *Complot contra la Iglesia* [Plot against the Church], whose author hides behind a pseudonym: Maurice Pinay. The image of the "Talmudic plot" was retaken

Fips
„Die Taufe hat aus ihm keinen Nichtjuden gemacht..."

14. Fips, pseudonym of Philipp Rupprecht, drawing published in Ernst Ludwig Hiemer's book *Der Giftpilz* [The Poisonous Mushroom]. *Der Stürmer*, Germany, 1938. United States Holocaust Memorial Museum. Collections: 1988.25.1. Available at: https://collections.ushmm.org/search/catalog/pa1069708. Access: 06.08.2019.

and Pope John XXIII was accused of being vulnerable to the powerful loggias and synagogues around the world.

An example of the persistence of the myth can be read on the pages of a pamphlet published in Argentina by Viejo Camarada Marcelino del Apuntador, entitled "La Masonería en Acción contra la Iglesia Católica" [Masonry in Action against the Catholic Church][56]. The article displays on the first page an illustration taken from the Nazi book for children written by Elvira Bauer, entitled *Trau keinem Fuchs auf grüner Heid und keinem Jud auf seinem Eid* [Trust no Fox on his Green Heath and no Jew on his Oath]. On the image, a fat Jew, dressed in tails and galley, seduces an Aryan woman by introducing himself as a gallant Catholic. The subtitle in the text by Viejo Camarada explains: "Argentina was captivated and seduced by them. They do it from the satanic low-life hangouts they have created."[57]

In that text, "Viejo Camarada" [Old Comrade] reproduces accusations that the "anti-Christian wrath of Freemasonry", assisted by Satan, acts in several countries among which he mentions Argentina, Chile, the United States and Mexico. The author reproduces slogans that instigated publications in France and Spain from the late 19th century, and took back the content of the book *La Franc-Maçonerie, Synagogue de Satan* [Frenchmasonry, Synagogue of Satan] (1893). There, the "Masonic work" is defined as "nefarious", marked by fanaticism and superstition against the Catholic Church, an action that he claims is visible in schools where crucifixes, catechisms and images of saints were suppressed, as well as the "holy name of

---

56 The pamphlet is available at: https://likedoc.org/the-philosophy-of-money.html?utm_source=la-masoneria-en-accion-contra-la-iglesia-catolica . Retrieved: Feb. 19, 2019.

57 *Ibidem.*

15. Demonization of the Jew. Page from the German antisemitic children's book "Trau Keinem Fuchs..." [Trust No Fox in The Green Meadow and No Jew on his Oath], by Elvira Bauer – *Der Stürmer*. Germany, 1936. United States Holocaust Memorial Museum. Available at: https://collections.ushmm.org/search/catalog/pa1069743. Access: 10.08.2019.

God and Jesus Christ". The author compares Chilean Freemasonry with the Grand Orient of France and concludes: "a foreign Occult Power, by means of the Chilean *loggias,* is leading much of our national life". In short, the lie, like the figure of Satan, survives in the collective imaginary, now in digital version.

MYTH 3

The Jews Dominate the World Economy

The myth says that Jews dominate the world economy. This economic slogan is directly connected to the involvement of Jews with the emergence of capitalism in the modern world in general, and in the American world in particular. It also intertwines with the thesis that Jews want to dominate the world, imposing themselves on all sectors of society: economy, politics, the press, education, etc.

The direct relationship between Jews and modern capitalism has brought about a collection of accusations from those who, due to envy or feeling stranded by the rules of their own religions, do not accept the conquests of this group in the business realm. For some of them, those who live as merchants or bankers do so "at the expense of others", and are seduced by greed, leisure and profit. However, the proclivity toward greed and ambition in human beings is not an exclusive "affliction" of Jews or capitalists.

The question goes beyond those feelings and points to an ethical stance of character, valid for all humanity, independent of beliefs, nationality, ideology or ethnicity. Hence the importance of education which, by means of knowledge, can integrate young people into an ethical and political dimension, guiding them to live in a diverse world, without prejudices. Such concerns range from *The Republic* by Plato (427–247 BCE) to *The New Testament*, from texts by the great Renaissance philosopher and humanist Thomas Moore (1478–1535), to those by German philosopher and revolutionary Karl Marx (1818–1883) or German sociologist Max Weber (1864–1920), among others.

Max Weber, in his classic work *The Protestant Ethic and the Spirit of Capitalism* (Die protestantische Ethik und der Geist des Kapitalismus), written between 1904 and 1905, helps us evaluate the extent of this myth, analyzed in the context of the radical transformations, operated by the Industrial Revolution, on man's material life. In his analysis of the origins of capitalism, Weber links some Old Testament norms to the ideal of justice and to the Jewish and Puritan ethic. From his point of view, the conception of professional vocation and an ascetic behavior, both practiced by Protestants and Jews, influenced the capitalist lifestyle. Asceticism consists in the methodical and continuous effort which, assisted by grace, promotes the full development of a spiritual life, applying the means to overcome obstacles. In this regard, Jews value the rational use of possessions, reinvestment in business and restless professional work as well as the "maintenance and continuity of hard work that pleases God".[58]

Max Weber acknowledges the fact that certain religions – such as Protestantism and Judaism – guide people in their everyday lives, and in economic practices in particular. Apparently, by being more prone to progress, they encourage their followers to pursue profit as a natural, vocation-driven pursuit. Such a stance – especially in the West – is driven by a force he calls "the spirit of modern capitalism", outlined by a

58 Max Weber, *The Protestant Ethic and the Spirit of Capitalism*, London and New York, Routledge, 2005.

particular ethos. That ethos is built by innovative individuals who have the qualities to rid themselves of the traditionalist thinking that treats them as "greedy beings". Weber emphasizes that both Protestants and Jews are endorsed by the ethics of their religions, to treat business as something natural, indispensable and essential to life, which is opposite to the stance of those who proclaim that individuals must work only to placate their basic needs. Therefore, for modern capitalism to work, an innovative behavior is necessary, as is a constant belief that, instead of a sin, following one's vocation is ethical and worthy of God's admiration. In that direction – that of a sinful, unethical misconduct, abusive of their power – follows the myth that Jews "dominate the world economy".[59]

This view of the world is contrary to the ethics defended by Catholicism, for example, which considers that obtaining profit by charging interest is a sin. With the advent of the Protestant Reformation, German monk Martin Luther protested various points in the doctrine of the Roman Catholic Church by publishing his 95 theses at the door of the Wittenberg Castle Church on October 31, 1517. Luther heeded the wishes of the bourgeoisie – who desired high economic gains, a practice condemned by Catholic ethics – and also of a nobility interested in seizing the Roman Church and ridding itself of the Papal taxes, which, despite the Church's proclamation of poverty and simplicity, was (and still is) the richest religious institution in the Western world. That new ethical conduct – the Protestant ethic – brought about changes: although it was not favorable to the accumulation of capital, it innovated through ideas about the division of labor and the will to progress as being "actions that observed God's will: it is the

59 *Ibidem.*

search for a state of grace; it is the individual exercising his or her vocation reserved to him by God". Weber seeks to demonstrate that work that leads to enrichment is allowed by Protestant ethics, which is rational in nature: "What God demands is not labor in itself, but rational labor in a calling".[60] For Protestantism, what counts is not the work itself but rational professional work, for that is exactly what God demands. That is: the believer must seize the opportunity to make profit in order to fulfill God's will with it.

For Werner Sombart, author of *The Apogee of Capitalism*, the origins of commercial or mercantile capitalism are strongly associated with the cities of Catholic tradition. In his opinion, which differs from Max Weber's, the Catholic Church played an important and active role in shaping the banking system. He considers influential the recommendations of Thomas Aquinas who minimizes the opposition between wealth and poverty and only considers to be sinful the "misuse" of wealth. According to Sombart, Protestantism had a decisive influence on industrial capitalism and Judaism pioneered in the development of the capitalist spirit. Hence, Jews do not defend any ascetic ideal of poverty, even though there are many poor Jews; they are excellent merchants and financiers, perhaps because they do not place restrictions on lending money to foreigners. Aware of the role of advertising and competition as being "the soul of business", they have always made good use of practicing discount prices, payments in installments with the charge of interests, both strategies commonly used to attract customers.[61] However, for the antisemite who is convinced that "Jews have no scruples"

---

60 *Idem.*, p. 107.

61 Werner Sombart, *El Apogeo del Capitalismo*, México, Fondo de Cultura Económica, 1984, 2 vols.

(read, ethic), such practice is criminal and it applies to all Jews. Catholics, Protestants, neo-Pentecostalists, evangelicals, and others would be exempt of this accusation. But not always . . .

In the blog www.inacreditavel.com.br, there is a text published in May 2013, signed by Norberto Toedter (a Holocaust denier), that takes up the same myth and enlarges it to other forces that, according to the author, would be trying to establish a New World Order. He prompts his readers to remember that Germany in the 1930s "identified what was going on at the world's backstage and . . . gave them a name: Plutocrats!". While confessing that "it is a big mistake to insist on the opposition between Nazis and Jews", Toedter declares that such an approach only serves to divert attention from the true manipulators of the world's destinies:

> Among them are not only the Rothschilds, Warburgs, Baruchs, Morgans [*sic*] but also the Rockefellers, who are evangelicals and many others who do not belong to the confession of the former. They are owners of banks, oil companies, publishing houses, kings, queens, heads of state. They possess, especially, a lot of money. They are capitalists or, as defined by a great expert in social communication of long ago, PLUTOCRATS. Their decisions are taken in meetings such as the Bilderberger, the Trilateral Commission, the Council on Foreign Relations, the Roundtable. Interesting for us is the fact that no South American names are on the membership lists. Will it do any good to believe that the pre-salt deposits will be ours?[62]

62 Norberto Toedter, who wrote . . . *E a Guerra Continua,* denies the Holocaust and keeps the blog *Inacreditável* [Italics is ours]. Retrieved on May 17, 2013: http://inacreditavel.com.br/wp/plutocratas/.

I use here the blog's name itself, which displays an exclamation mark: Inacreditável! [Unbelievable!]. It is indeed unbelievable that accusations like those can still find followers and readers in the 21st century.

The Semitic Danger as a Global Concern

In order to understand the dynamics of the myth that "Jews dominate the world economy", and its extension throughout the twentieth and twenty-first centuries, we must take up the history of the *Protocols* which, as a product of various political myths, became one of the driving forces behind modern antisemitism and genocide. Its content takes us back to another related myth: that the Jews constitute an international secret society, they control the media and politics, they finance wars and weapons trafficking, etc. That work, which is considered one of the greatest forgeries in contemporary history, is the perfect example of the principle that when a lie is repeated countless times, no matter how ridiculous it is, it begins to be accepted as a truth.

The matrix that gave rise to the *Protocols* was inspired by the work written at the end of the 19th century by Sergei Nilus who, in turn, based his text on a satire published in Brussels (1864), authored by Maurice Joly, against Napoleon III, the Emperor of France entitled *Dialogue aux Enfers: Machiavel et Montesquieu* [Dialogues in Hell: Machiavelli and Montesquieu]. It reconstitutes a dialogue between Machiavelli and Montesquieu in hell, and displays Napoleon as a cynical, greedy, unscrupulous and adventurous man, whose ambition was to seize power and broaden the conquests initiated by his uncle Napoleon I. Two years later, the lectures were republished under the title *The Root of Our Troubles: Where the Root of Current*

Society Disorders is Found in Europe and Especially in Russia.[63] In 1905, the year of the first Russian revolt (theme of the movie The Battleship Potemkin, directed by Sergei Eisenstein), Sergei Aleksandrovich Nilus published the book *The Great within the Small and Antichrist, an Imminent Political Possibility. Notes by an Orthodox Believer*, in which *The Protocols* were included. Even today, this is the version that serves as a matrix for the printed editions of the *Protocols* in various parts of the world. Although this hoax was denounced in 1921 by a *The Times'* correspondent in London, it continues to proliferate and win over followers.

In this context, one must not underestimate the power of the myth and its constant capacity to update and revitalize itself: in 1898, the French caricaturist C. Léandre created a political cartoon whose title was "Rothschild" which was reproduced in 1921 by Eduard Fucks (1870–1940) in his book *Die Juden in der Karicatur ein Beitrag zur Kulturgeschichte*. This image foreshadowed many others that would be published during the first half of the 20th century. Here one can once again see the stereotypical figure of the Jew with a hooked nose and raptor claws embracing the world. Over the crown, the figure of a golden calf protrudes over a golden halo that reads "Israel".

In 1906, Georgy Butmi[64] – based on Nilus's text, which was inspired by Maurice Joly's novel – drew up a new edition with small alterations in the text and published *Enemies of the Human Race: Protocols Extracted from the Secret Archives of the Central Chancellery of Zion*. The essence of the arguments is centered on the idea that "the ancient sages" conspired in Zion, formu-

63 Pierre-André Taguieff, *Les Protocoles des Sages de Sion*, vol. 1: Introduction à l'étude des Protocoles: um faux et ses usages dans le siècle, Paris, Berg International, 1992.

64 Curta biografia.

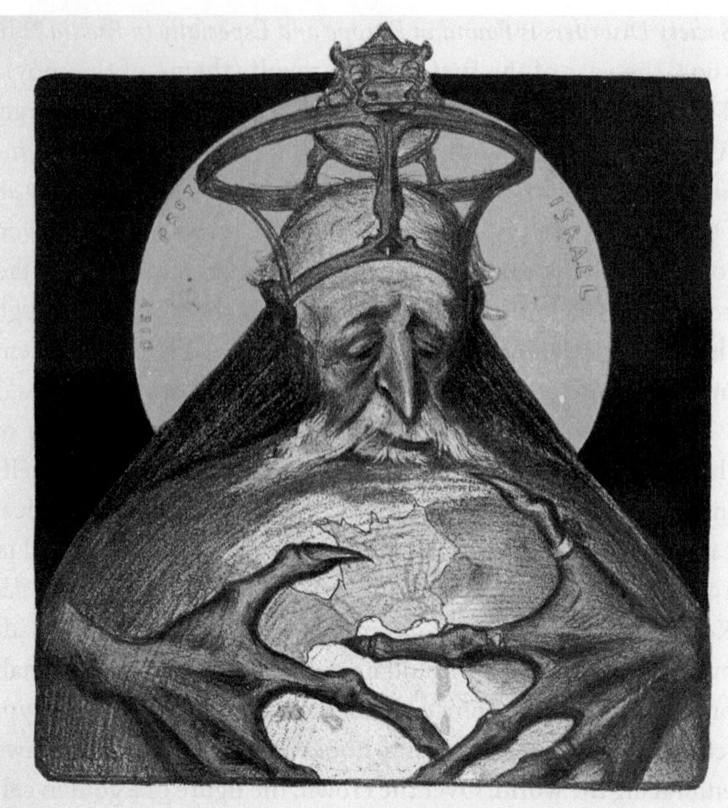

16. C. Léandre. French caricaturista, author of the political cartoon entitled "Rothschild", 1898, published in Eduard Fuchs, "Die Juden in der Karikatur: ein Beitrag zur Kulturgeschichte", Munich, Albert Langen, 1921. United States Holocaust Memorial Museum. Available at: https://collections.ushmm.org/search/catalog/pa1041697. Access: 10.08.2019.

lating a secret plan to destroy the Christian world. From that date onwards we have seen the multiplication of a lie that, throughout the 20th century, was enriched with new additions taken from the realities of the world: economic crises, unemployment, terrorism, illegal immigration, AIDS, etc.

In 1919, another expanded version of the *Protocols* emerged in Germany, translated by Gottfried zur Beck, who inserted new fragments into the original work produced in Tsarist Russia. He updated it with information about World War I, the Russian Revolution of 1917, the German defeat, etc. The narrative was (re)constructed to induce the reader to believe that Jews were a secret society and plotted to dominate the world. The conspiracy theory gained strength with other fragments added by zur Beck, copied from a vulgar pamphlet authored by Herman Goedsche, who also dealt with the subject of the Jewish conspiracy. Thus, the myth became popular throughout Germany in inexpensive, "pocket book" editions. During the 1920s to 1940s, it got a Polish translation, followed by several editions, being three French, one British, three American, one Scandinavian, one Italian and one Japanese. At the same time, *The Times* proclaimed the existence of such a conspiracy by means of 23 editorials published by *The Morning Post* as a book entitled *The Cause of World Restlessness.* Even after that, the truthfulness of the *Protocols* was not affected or, much less, extinguished the limelight given to them by Nazism.[65]

Between 1919 and 1921, impressed with the content of the Protocols, Henry Ford founded a magazine to make them known to the American public: *The Dearborn Independence-Trade Union,* also known as *The Ford International Weekly,* which circulated until 1927. The newspaper reached nearly three thousand subscribers, a large part of whom belonged to the American Jewish community and were concerned about the proliferation of the defamatory myth. That same year, Ford

65 On this polemic, see W. Creutz, "A Autenticidade dos Protocolos dos Sábios de Sião", in *Os Protocolos dos Sábios de Sião*. Coleção Comemorativa do Centenário de Gustavo Barroso, Porto Alegre, Editora Revisão, 1989, p. 43.

published the book *The International Jew,* whose circulation reached 150,000 copies and, with the same intention, Theodor Fritsch printed another magazine in Germany, *Der International Jude.* Those means, helped the myth to conquer new readers, fueled by the ideas of an international conspiracy and of a Jewish-communist conspiracy.[66]

Those pamphlets served to multiply the lie: it echoed along National Socialists who, even before Hitler's rise to power, sought to justify the repression of the Jews under the pretext that they wanted to dominate the world's economy. From the party's birth in the early 1920s, the accusations revealed by the *Protocols* found in Alfred Rosenberg (1893–1946) – the party's ideologue on racial issues and a confidant of Adolf Hitler – a source of propaganda.[67]

The accusation that Jews dominated the world's economy was transformed into fantasy and became an obsession to Rosenberg and Hitler, which served to justify, among many other elements, the extermination of millions of Jews and other ethnic and political groups, a genocidal action that culminated in the Final Solution. According to Norman Cohn, a scholar devoted to the study of the myth of the world Jewish

---

66 Maria Luiza Tucci Carneiro, *O Veneno da Serpente. Reflexões sobre o Moderno Anti-semitismo no Brasil,* São Paulo, Perspectiva, 2003, pp. 52–57; *O Anti-semitismo nas Américas, op. cit.*

67 In 2013, Rosenberg's personal diary was found in the United States between 1936 and 1944. Besides being a party ideologue, Rosenberg directed the Nazi plunder of the artistic, cultural and religious heritage of the Jews throughout Europe by means of the *Reichsleiter* Rosenberg Task Force Unit. He was convicted of crimes against humanity and executed in October 1946. See *Folha de S. Paulo,* June 10, 2013. http://www1.folha.uol.com.br/mundo/2013/06/1292879-eua-encontram-diario-perdido-de-lider-nazista-alfred-rosenberg.shtml

conspiracy, Rosenberg published five pamphlets between 1919 and 1923 that, in addition to being widely disseminated among the German population, had a strong influence on the way Germans viewed Jews: as a plague to be exterminated. One of those pamphlets – *Pest in Russland* [Plague in Russia] (1922) – asserted that hatred against the Jews in Tsarist Russia had come about because of their connections to financial capitalism. In that text, the argument remains that Jews, "by means of their dialectical skills applied during centuries of commentary, through the Talmud, convinced the Russian population to contend against the national elites and took over the Russian industry which brought great wealth to them".[68]

Rosenberg assigns a special role to Walter Rathenau, who he accused of maintaining a close relationship with Bolshevik Jews from the Soviet Union who, in turn, shared with him the riches that they extracted from the Russian industry. By making some kind of "apocalyptic prophecy", Rosenberg manages to link that group to the Chinese silk merchants who, together with the Latvians, had supposedly tried to subjugate the Russians and Germans to capitalism. Announcing the beginning of a *new era free of Jews,* Rosenberg proposes as a "vanguard sign for the next struggle towards a new world organization: the understanding of their devilish character and the fight against world domination by the Jews, up to the attainment of a vigorous rebirth, and the unleashing of the nets threaded by the Talmudic *trappers* who, like the phoenix, rise from the ashes of a materialistic philosophy already burned, buried".[69]

---

68 Norman Cohn, *El Mito de la conspiración judía mundial: Los Protocolos de los Sabios de Sión,* Madrid, Alianza Editorial, 1983, pp. 216–218.

69 *Idem,* p. 218.

Thus, both Alfred Rosenberg and Josef Goebbels, the Party's head of propaganda since 1928, articulated a discourse based on deliberate lies, accusing Jews of enslaving the German people, of being plutocrats and monopolists, of exploiting others. In other words, Nazi Germany appropriated the content of the *Protocols* to justify the expansion of their living space towards Eastern European countries as well as the extermination of Jews, many of whom were fully integrated into German society. Hitler, during his jail time in Landsberg (1924–1926), sought to systematize his hatred against the Jews by packing it as a doctrine. It was inside the prison that the future Führer created *Mein Kampf* which, together with the *Protocols,* became the Bible of the Nazis and antisemites. In his work, Hitler invokes the myth of a secret conspiracy devised by the Wise Men of Zion, a text that fed the type of antisemitism propagated by the German state and served to justify, among other writings, the measures of exception and extermination against the Jews in the 1930s and 1940s in Germany. It suffices to revisit the discourse propagated by the Third Reich (1933–1945) to evaluate the escalation of that hatred: allegedly, Germany needed to be "free of Jews" (*Judenrein*), since they were the ones who had "Bolshevized the country by way of Weimar's social-democracy". Identified as allies of the communists, the Jews, day after day, were accused of exploiting and enslaving the people to foreign bankers.

As we have already said, the political myth is (re)fueled by the reality to construct a new version that mobilizes less well-informed people, who are seduced by the antisemitic propaganda, as was the case in Nazi Germany. There are actually countless examples of Jewish bankers who, after World War I and during the Weimar Republic, tried to help Germany to overcome the crisis that resulted from the war reparations imposed by the Treaty of Versailles (1919).[70] According to Jacques Attali, author of the book *The Jews, Money and the World*, published in 2010, one of the country's top bankers, Max Warburg, for example, financed "the acquisition of new ships for a shipping line he helped to save from bankruptcy, and also avoided, in compliance with the rules imposed by the Treaty of Versailles, the confiscation of the subsidiaries of Zeiss and Krupp abroad, which were then concealed as British and Dutch companies, after their acquisition by Warburg who opened branches in London and Amsterdam.[71] In that intermission, several Jews rose to important positions during the Weimar Republic (1919–1933); even its constitution was written by Hugo Preuss, a Jewish lawyer. An important role was played by Kurt Eisner (1867–1919), a descendant of Jews named Kamonowsky, a leading figure in the German Independent Social Democratic Party, alongside Karl Kautsky, Eduard Bernstein, Julius Leber, Rudolf Breitscheild and Rudolf Hilferding.

In the 1920s, Germany was deeply in debt and a large part of the population was starving and living in misery. In 1921, the official value of war reparations to be paid by Germany was stipulated: 33 million dollars. From that year onwards, Germany's political and economic climate favored the "a hunt for Jews":

---

70 The main point of the Treaty of Versailles was that Germany accepted all responsibility for having caused the war and, under the terms of Articles 231–247, determined that she paid reparations to several nations of the Triple Entente. The terms imposed to Germany included the loss of part of its territory to several bordering countries, restricted the size of the army and required compensation for damages caused during the war. In Germany, the treaty caused shock and humiliation to the population, an element that would later contribute to the fall of the Weimar Republic in 1933 and the rise of Nazism.

71 Jacques Attali, *Les juifs, le monde et l'argent*, Paris, Le Livre de Poche, 2003.

Kurt Eisner was assassinated in 1919 and Walther Rathenau, the Foreign Affairs Minister, was killed in June 1922, by members of the Consul, a nationalist and antisemitic secret organization.

After 1922, most German banks were on the brink of bankruptcy and leaders of the Weimar Republic were accused of having failed to mitigate the effects of the reparations imposed by the Treaty of Versailles. The situation of crisis favored an inversion of values that would pave the way for antisemitic virulence. Some bankers were enriched through speculation and manipulation of the financial market, strengthening the myth that Jews dominated the economy, money and the world, and that "every road lead to the Rothschilds". Actually, this would be one of the most cited names by antisemitic fanatics and continues to function as a "trigger for the most explosive antisemitic tremors", according to a 2000 report by the *Anti-Defamation League*.[72]

The House of Warburg survived thanks to loans granted by the Kuhn-Loeb Bank, which had connections to the House of Rothschild. In September 1923, Paul and Max Warburg succeeded in creating the Hamburger Bank, which issued its own banknotes anchored in the Kuhn-Loeb fund. In November, Gustav Stresemann's government implemented a new currency in Germany, the *Rentenmark*, backed by a set of assets linked to the German economy. In addition, negotiations on the issue of reparations and the inflow of American capital by means of loans

---

72 Fritz Springmeier, "The Power of the Rotschilds", in http://rense.com/general77/powers.htm, retrieved on May 11, 2018. ADL, Anti-Defamation League, "Jewish Control of the Federal Reserve: A Classic Anti-Semitic Myth", https://www.adl.org/resources/backgrounders/jewish-control-of-the-federal-reserve-a-classic-anti-semitic-myth#introduction, retrieved on May 11, 2018.

implemented by the *Dawes Plan* in 1924, which helped to bring a certain financial stability to the country that, slowly, stared to be rebuilt and later became one of the world's major industrial nations. Before 1933, firms such as Siemens, Hapag, Vereignite Sahlwerk and IG Farben were already known for their economic power.[73]

During this *interregnum*, the Jews – increasingly integrated, especially by means of mixed marriage – had lost key positions in the banking and industrial sector, holding only the Deutsche Bank, led by Oscar Wasserman, and Jacob Godlschmidt's Darmstädter Bank.[74] Between 1925 and 1929, the phantasmagoric unemployment figure delineated a Germany divided between a rich minority and the majority of an unemployed population, a situation that paved the way for the rise to power of the National Socialists and to the spread of antisemitism. In 1925, the city of Berlin had about 120,000 unemployed people. This number jumped to 284,000 in January 1927 and to half a million in 1929. In 1932 – the year Hitler was beaten in the elections by von Hindenburg – the country, according to historian Frederic Ewen, had surpassed the record figure of six million unemployed.[75] Between 1933 and 1945, the antisemitic

---

73 See Frederic Ewen. *Brecht. Sua Vida. Sua Arte. Seu Tempo*, São Paulo, Editora Globo, 1991, p. 128

74 Jacques Attali, *op. cit.*, pp. 496–497.

75 *Idem*, p. 239. See Maurini de Souza's interesting analysis of the advertisements that, in the interwar period, were used to entertain the German elite. Maurini de Souza, "A trajetória do Tratamento de Segunda Pessoa em Textos Publicitários durante o Século XX: Um Comparativo entre Brasil e Alemanha", Doctoral Thesis, Linguistic Studies Program, Department of Human Sciences, Letters and Arts, Curitiba, Federal University of Paraná, 2012, pp. 195–196. Available at: https://acervodigital.ufpr.br/bitstream/handle/1884/26951/VERSAO%20FINAL.pdf?sequence=1. Retrieved: May 11, 2018

discourse triggered by the Third Reich upheld the thesis that Jews were "guilty of all evils" that afflicted the German Nation.

The concern about Jewish world domination of the economy survived World War II, given that some Jewish banks survived – although also Catholic, Protestant, and many others did so as well. The Rothschilds remained dominant in Britain, while Horace Finaly held the presidency of the Banque de Paris et de Pays-Bas. The economic success of those leaders contributes to the rehabilitation of the myth, as we can see in the book *Called to Serve* by Colonel James "Bo" Gritz, a candidate to the US presidency in 1992 on the Populist Party's ticket. Recurring to the old antisemitic slogan, James Gritz – who during his campaign openly called on the United States to become a Christian nation – denounced that "eight Jewish families control the Federal Reserve System (FED)". In 1983, the National Association of Retired Federal Employees (NARFE), in Pennsylvania, published in its newsletter that the Federal Reserve System was a "private company" controlled by the following banks: Rothschild in London and Berlin, the Lazard brothers – Banque de Paris– in France, Israel Moses Seif in Italy, Warburg in Hamburg and Amsterdam, Lehman Bros., Chase Manhattan Bank, Kuhn, Loeb & Co., Bank of New York, Goldman Sachs in the US. That is what the myth said, but the truth is different. In 1995 and again in 2000, the Anti-Defamation League denounced such accusation as "a classic example of the myth", reporting that, except for the Chase Manhattan Bank, none of the institutions cited in the NARFE bulletin were members of the Federal Reserve Bank of New York, the largest and most important of the twelve FED banks.[76]

76 ADL, "Jewish Control of the Federal Reserve: A Classic Anti-Semitic Myth", *op. cit.*

The Myth in Brazil

In 1930s Brazil, the myth that the Jews dominated the world's economy had influential proponents, including integralists Gustavo Barroso, Brasilino de Carvalho and Tenório d'Albuquerque, all inspired by 19th and 20th century French and German matrices, respectively. Those integralist intellectuals had as their main readings the apocryphal work *The Protocols of the Elders of Zion* and *The International Jew* by Henry Ford, as recorded in their numerous bibliographical citations. In the 1930s, during the Vargas administration, *Editorial Globo*, a publisher house from Porto Alegre, in Southern Brazil, published the first integralist texts, which sought, by use of "explanatory notes", to attract Brazilian readers for *The Protocols*. Thus, the myth of the Jewish plot broadened its accusations, and also served the *myth of the international communist plot*, which spread among followers of Nazi-fascist and anti-communist ideologies, mobilized by nationalist, xenophobic and antisemitic sentiments. A similar phenomenon occurred in Nazi Germany, Fascist Italy, Salazarist Portugal, Francoist Spain, Peronist Argentina and Getulist Brazil. In all those countries, the climate was favorable for the indication of a culprit for the constant crises that afflicted their populations. The Jews immediately emerged as the target enemy, and were held accountable for all the chaos, as well as for the political and financial instability.[77]

---

77 Luis Reis Torgal and Heloisa Paulo (orgs.), *Estados Autoritários e Totalitários e suas Representações*, Coimbra, Imprensa da Universidade de Coimbra, 2008; Carlos Cordeiro (org.), *Autoritarismo, Totalitarismo e Respostas Democráticas*, Coimbra, CEIS20, Ponta Delgada, Centro de Estudos Gaspar Frutuoso, Universidade dos Açores, 2011; Federico Croci and Maria Luiza Tucci Carneiro (orgs.), *Tempos de Fascismos, São Paulo*, Edusp, Imprensa Oficial, Arquivo Público do Estado, 2011.

In every country where the *Protocols* circulated, they emerged as the code for the Antichrist, having as their interpreters an intellectual elite identified with the ideology of the extreme right, both Catholic and nationalist. Despite doubts, the *Book of the Wise Men of Zion*, was widely disseminated in Brazil by Catholic newspapers, such as *Vozes de Petrópolis* and the integralist newspaper *Acção*, published in São Paulo. In 1937, the Protocols reached their third Brazilian edition with a print run of 23,000 copies, apart from many clandestine editions and some commemorative ones replicated until 1995, disguised in several forms.

In 1938, integralist Gustavo Barroso wrote Roosevelt, *é Judeu* (Roosevelt, is a Jew), which was translated into Spanish by Mario Buzatto and published in Argentina in the *Cuadernos Antijudíos* [Anti-Jewish Notebooks], in support for a strong antisemitic campaign in that country. According to Hector de Herze, who introduced the reader to the subject, Gustavo Barroso was hated by the "synagogue" for having discovered that Getúlio Vargas's opponent, a candidate for the Presidency of the Republic in 1937, was a Jew who hid his maternal surname (Moretzohn) under the Portuguese surname Armando Salles de Oliveira. The myth resumed some of his arguments to explain the arrest of several integralists in 1938, after a *coup* attempt by "green shirts" led by Plínio Salgado: the repression of integralists was explained as a demonstration of "*the hidden power* of the Kahal", a maneuver of Judaism allied to the Masonic *loggias*.[78]

The Semitic danger came into play again, a transvestite of modernity and interpreted under the prism of capitalism as an

---

78 Gustavo Barroso, *Roosevelt, é Judeu*, traducción de Mario Buzatto e introducción de Héctor de Herze, Buenos Aires, La Mazorca, 1938 (Cuadernos Antijudíos).

17. GA.G., author of the demonized image of the Jews that illustrates the cover of Oswaldo Gouveia's *Os Judeus do Cinema* [The Jews of the Cinema].]. I have not been able to identify who the initials belong to. Rio de Janeiro, Graphica São Jorge, 1935. Tucci Collection/ State of São Paulo/Brazil.

economic system that destroys humanity. In some publications that circulated in Brazil in the 1930s, the *Protocols* were recommended particularly to bank employees characterized as "poor bank workers". The Jewish or Semitic danger was animalized and introduced as a "seven-headed monster" that wants to swallow the people. Such images satisfied (and still satisfy) the fantasy-minded readers of antisemitic works that they do not need to see in order to believe. The metaphors facilitate the circulation of the myth distilled by cartoonists, caricaturists and literary writers who, by means of images and literary texts, transform Jews into monsters, poisonous reptiles, hydras with many heads, spiders, octopuses and snakes. Over the years, gradually and subtly, minds are forged through the introduction of intimidating characters, inciting hatred and repulsion towards the Jewish people.

In 1934, a popular edition of *The Protocols* was published in France under the title of *Le Péril Juif*. Its cover portrays an old Jew who, with his long nails on a globe, plucks blood from the world. At the base of this image there are bodies supposedly massacred due to Jewish gain. That same iconic narrative inspired the cover of *O Anti-Semitismo de Hitler e o Julgamento Apressado de Alguns Escriptores Brasileiros* [Hitler's Antisemitism and the Hasty Trial by some Brazilian Writers] by Brasilino de Carvalho, published in Bahia in 1934.[79] Most of the images it contains seek to express how Jews pursue profit and domination of the economy, through representations of a purse either with a monetary sign stamped on it or stuffed with coins that are also spread on the floor; a depiction inherited from the legendary figure of Judas.

In some publications, the artist/caricaturist seeks to attribute a Jewish identity to the "greedy" character who, in that context, seeks to dominate, explore others and control the world: he includes a seven-armed golden candelabra (the *Menorah*) or a Star of David, and appeals to the black garments commonly worn by orthodox Jews, usually placing them, almost always, behind the image of a globe. The words applied on the covers or used in titles of chapters reinforce the idea of a supposed Jewish domination: liberalism, autonomy, laws, gold, politics, faith, power, trade, crisis, religions, etc. The body

79 *Le Péril Juif: Les Protocoles des Sages de Sion*, Paris, Les Nouvelles Editions Nationales, 1934; Brasilino de Carvalho, *O Anti-semitismo de Hitler . . . E o Julgamento Apressado de Alguns Escritores Brasileiros*, Bahia, 1934.

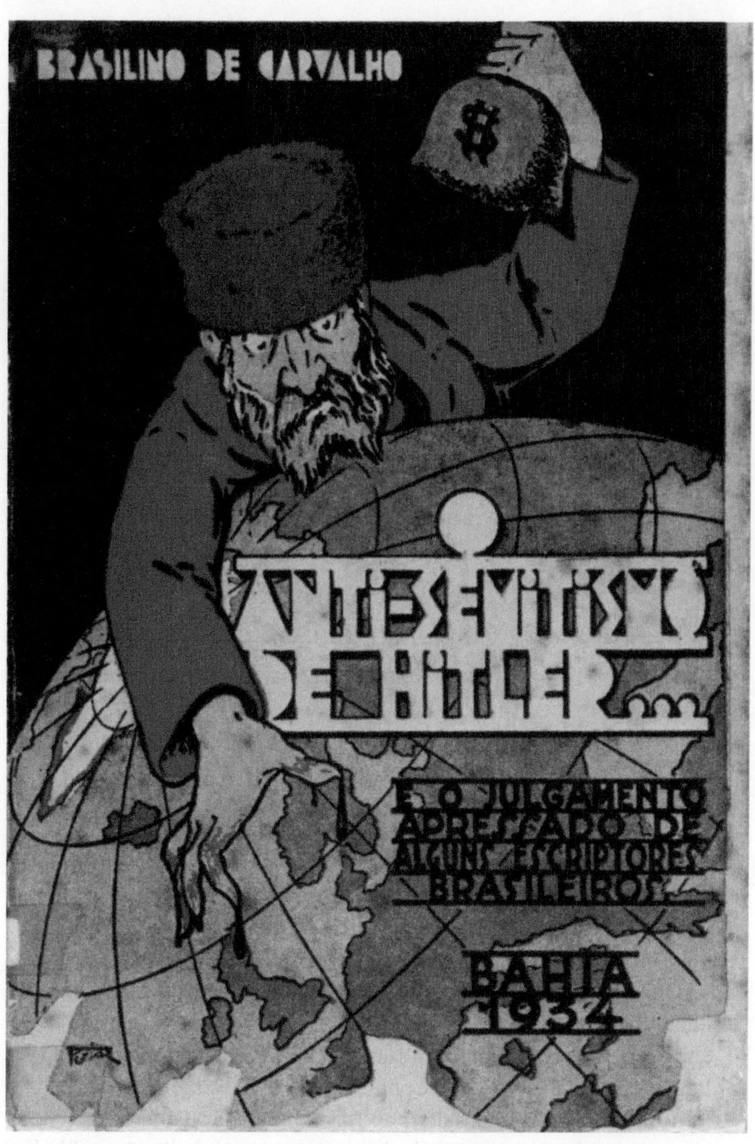

18. Unidentified author. Stigmatized image of the Jew represented as a communist, bloodthirsty and greedy. Cover of the book *O Anti-semitismo de Hitler* [Hitler's Antisemitism], by Brasilino de Carvalho. Bahia, s.e., 1934. Tucci Collection/ State of São Paulo/Brazil.

of those works, display commonplace statements explaining that the action of Jews to dominate the world is conducted according to the Talmud, defined as a "code of criminals". Integralist Gustavo Barroso, for example, paraphrasing the thought of French author L. Bertrand, affirms in his preface to "The Talmud and the Jews", that via the Jewish religious and moral guide, the non-Jewish (the *goy*) would be able to understand the desires and the disguised actions of Judaism. Barroso's argument is structured around several decontextualized fragments from the Talmud, in which he seeks to demonstrate the "infamy of a parasitic people who are governed by a code of that order". He accuses Judaism of being clumsy, usurer, thief, murderer of peoples, and proclaims the authenticity of the *Protocols*.[80]

Barroso takes up once again the accusation that the Jews dominate the world economy in his book *Sinagoga Paulista*, published in 1937, amid a period in Brazil called *Estado Novo* [New State].[81] His goal was to prove that São Paulo was being

80 L. Bertrand, *Maçonaria, Seita Judaica: Suas Origens, Sagacidade e Finalidade Anti-cristãs*, I. ed. 1903, translation and foreword by Gustavo Barroso, São Paulo, Minerva, 1938, pp. 5–9.

81 Estado Novo: a period governed by Getúlio Vargas, that began with the *coup d'etat* of November 10, 1937 and finished with Vargas' deposition on October 29, 1945. It is characterized as a dictatorship for its ideals inspired by the paradigms of the fascist regimes in vogue in Europe and identified by systematic manifestations of xenophobia, racism and exacerbated nationalism. By means of a repressive apparatus, the state imposed a tight control of the population, which was inhibited by censorship and by actions of a political police dedicated to the repression of communists and ethnic minorities, including Jews, Blacks and Japanese, who were classified as undesirable. Between 1937 and 1945, the Vargas government issued Secret Memoranda aimed at preventing the entry of Jewish refugees from Nazism, a stance that was maintained during the rule of Eurico Gaspar Dutra (1946–1950).

19. *Brasil, Colônia de Banqueiros*, by Gustavo Barroso. Rio de Janeiro, Civilização Brasileira, 2nd ed., 1934. Cover. Tucci Collection/ State of São Paulo/Brazil.

dominated by a "synagogue of Judaized, Judaizers and Jewish bankers". Exploring this plot – which had already been denounced by Henry Ford in The *International Jew* – he claimed that "hidden culprits" had ruined the coffee economy and impoverished the country. After listing the names of important Brazilian families, the author accuses them of serving the skillful maneuver of Jews who mobilize men and wage-earners through the practice of bribery and other illegal means. Repeating catch-phrases inspired by the *Protocols*, Barroso stated that Judaism in Brazil was linked to international Judaism, represented by the high-finance in London and that the downturn in the coffee economy would have been simulated by the *Sinagoga Paulista,* supported by the government. Both were allegedly obtaining high profits, thus demoralizing the coffee market.[82]

In meetings at the Brazilian Academy of Letters, academic Gustavo Barroso (who was also the director of the *Museu Nacional do Rio de Janeiro* [Rio de Janeiro National Museum], euphorically attacked the Israelites, calling them "human garbage". And on the front page of *A Ofensiva,* an integralist newspaper, he denounced as "Jewish" the impulses of businessman and economist Roberto Simonsen.[83] In 1991, an edition commemorating Gustavo Barroso's centenary in 1991, Editora Revisão – a publishing house in the Brazilian Southern city of Porto Alegre – defined integralists as those who who "laid bare the nefarious actions of financial Judaism in the country". In this publication, the myth that Jews dominate the world economy was updated by Siegfried Ellwanger Castan (1928–2010), a Brazilian revisionist editor and writer, who, in 1996, was convicted of the crime of racism by judges of the Third Criminal Chamber of the State of Rio Grande do Sul Court of Justice. In his book, Castan updated the myth, blaming Jews of forming cartels, among other accusations.[84]

In 1935, the stigmatized figure of the Jew reappeared in a masterful drawing by a cartoonist known as Belmonte, the pseudonym of Benedito Carneiro Bastos Barreto (1896–1947). In

---

82 Gustavo Barroso, *A Sinagoga Paulista,* 3rd ed., Rio de Janeiro, ABC, 1937, pp. 132, 135–155.

83 Entry "Gustavo Barroso", in *Dicionário Histórico-Biográfico Brasileiro.* Coord. Israel Beloch, Alzira Alves de Abreu, Rio de Janeiro, Forense Universitária, CPDOC/FGV, Finep, 1985, vol. 1, p. 336–337.

84 *Os Protocolos dos Sábios de Sião,* Coleção Comemorativa do Centenário de Gustavo Barroso, Porto Alegre, Revisão, 1989, p. 17 (1st re-edition 1991).

his work *Ideias de Ninguém*, published in 1935, Belmonte reaffirms the sinister figure of the Jew who, seated on a bag of coins, resembles a bat whose claws do not deny his intentions.[85] His booklet brings together some of the chronicles and images published by the cartoonist in the newspaper *Folha da Noite* in 1933 and 1934, followed by a brief history. Although the author claims that he had the "altruistic aim of distracting potential readers with cheerful comments about serious episodes that would have been buried in the common fence of newspaper collections", the result was not great. Referring to the peaceful "invasion" of Nazi antisemitism in France, Belmonte quotes the words by writer Clement Vautel, who said also "that the Jews are fomenting war and, when it explodes, they will exclaim: 'Aux armes, Français, allez délivrer nos frères!'"

Belmonte believed that, "where there is 'Semitism' – not as a racial denomination, but as a political expression – there should eventually and inexorably be 'antisemitism'", because "every action provokes a reaction". In any case, the truth is that the campaign against the Jews, which began in France, is one of the most disconcerting events in this bewildering cycle of confusion. In that sequence, he still comments:

> But the most complicated thing in all this is that the Jews of France are not just runaways from Germany. There are millions of them. And they do not mourn in *ghettos*. They dominate. So much so that Mr. Fougère sent an indication to the table about the case, in which he reads those comments that cause astonishment: "they (the Jews), in a

85 Belmonte [Benedito Carneiro Bastos Barreto], *Ideias de Ninguém*, Rio de Janeiro, Livraria José Olympio Editora, 1935. Electronic version eBooksBrasil, Digital Source.

20. Belmonte. *O perigo mysterioso...* [The Mysterious Danger]. Reproduced from his work *Ideias de Ninguém* [Ideas by No One], Rio de Janeiro, José Olympio Editora 1935. Version for eBooksBrasil, Digital Source.

> purpose contrary to the interests of the country and peace, exert influence on the direction of France's foreign policy and disorient public opinion with their propaganda and press campaigns".

It is still common to hear the accusation that a Jewish minority dominates the Brazilian banking sector, forgetting that there are other banking powers whose owners are mostly Catholic. Are there banks owned by Jews? Yes, indeed! But who are the other bankers? The version that persists is always widespread and tries to pass on the idea that we live in a "judeocracy in a democracy". Here is the fact: the myth lies and takes advantage of the plausibility attributed to a reality that carries an appearance (probability of truth). In other words, for the myth, everything is possible and such accusations are not examples from medieval times: they are out there, in the mouth of the uninformed, easy prey and prone to manipulation.

MYTH 4

There are no Poor Jews

The myth says that poor Jews do not exist. The narratives insist on the fact that most of them are rich, stingy and greedy, and relate that greed to the legendary figure of the Jewish usurer, popularly personified by the figure of Judas, the "traitor apostle" who gave up Jesus in exchange for thirty silver coins. The information omitted by the promoters of this myth is that there have always been poor Jews, middle-class Jews and rich Jews, such as is the case among Catholics, Protestants, Muslims and Evangelicals, who also have people in various economic and social positions. Lack of information leads to the proliferation of the myth that, when repeated, "makes us see what we are told". This being so, ignorance is an ideal condition for the development of racist myths.

By means of metaphors, I would like to emphasize here my conviction that education is the strategy to combat myths: ignorance is the incubator, the hot nest in which the snake lays its eggs of hatred and intolerance. However, the image that persists in the 21st century is that of the rich Jew. Those who are fond of this version generally ignore the historical circumstances that forced Jews to work with money matters. This is a topic that has been extensively addressed in a book by Algerian economist and author Jacques Attali *Les Juifs, le Monde et l'Argent, Histoire économique du peuple juif* [The Jews, the World and Money, an Economic History of the Jewish People].[86] Although I am aware of the danger posed by generalizations, I will seek here to contextualize – both historically and in the realm of political myths – the so-called "privileged position" that generally keeps the Jew out of the category of "poor".

Going back to the Roman Empire, especially between 135 and 425, we find that, both in the Diaspora and in Palestine, Jews always had diversified professions and occupations, working as traders, farmers, craftsmen. They could be found in every strata of society and, according to Marcel Simon in his work *Verus Israel* (1948), the Jewish population was formed by "a large majority of people of low income…".[87] It is estimated that, at that time, nearly one million Jews lived in Palestine and three to four million lived in the Diaspora, scattered from Asia Minor to Spain, and accounting for 7 to 8 percent of the total population of the Roman Empire.[88]

Until the 4th century, they were recognized as Roman citizens and enjoyed the privileges granted by the pagan emperors. For instance, they were authorized to keep their synagogues as spaces dedicated to worship. However, this situation changed and the Jewish community, due to the ecclesiastical influence on the Roman legislation, started to lose privileges and security. Those changes were present in the laws created under the Christian emperors since 312, which are compiled in the Theodosian Code (Codex Theodosianus). That year, Christianity was legalized, and became a major ally of the

86 Jacques Attali, *op. cit.*

87 Marcel Simon, *Verus Israel,* Paris, 1948, p. 241, cited by Léon Poliakov, *Du Christ aux Juifs de Cour, op. cit.*

88 Léon Poliakov, *Du Christ aux Juifs de Cour, op. cit.*, p. 5.

Roman emperors – the reason why it is interpreted, in the 4th century, as a framework in the history of Jewish–Christian relations. From that moment onwards, the situation of the Jews in the Roman Empire shifted, as a consequence of the Christian propaganda led by priests and religious fanatics. Over the course of a century, Jews went from the prosperity of the classical world to the poverty of the medieval ghetto, "from privileged citizens to outcasts", and, with a great deal of difficulty, were able to reconquer their rights and citizenship, according to the analysis of historian James Everett Seaver.[89]

During the Nazi era, a state-sponsored official propaganda re-emerged, accusing Jews of being guilty of all the ills that beset the nation. Hate was spread by claims that stated that all international bankers were Jews and that, even being rich, Jews went around dressed as poor, to deceive everyone. An example of this distortion is the image signed by the German caricaturist Fips, pseudonym of Philipp Rupprecht, the same illustrator of *Der Giftpilz* (The Poison Mushroom, by Ernst Ludwig Hiemer). On the upper left corner is the logo of the newspaper *Der Stürmer* and the message: "Without a solution to the Jewish question, there will be no salvation for humanity."

In that context, it is worth mentioning the important autobiographical novel, *Jews Without Money*, published in 1930 by American author Michael Gold,[90] whose parents emigrated to the United States fleeing the *pogroms*, in search for the American dream. Certainly, had the book fallen into the hands of a Nazi officer, its title would have resulted in a lot of laughter. Gold's almost poetic tale should be interpreted as a libel against Jewish

89 James Everett Seaver, *The Persecution of the Jews in the Roman Empire (300–428)*, Lawrence, Kansas, University of Kansas, 1952, pp. 4–5.

90 A pseudonym of Itzok Isaac Granich (1894–1967).

poverty as he experienced it during his childhood in a poor New York neighborhood at the beginning of the 20th century. His vision of the world was universal, while his work, *Jews without Money*, is timeless and fights discrimination against any people. In his notes, he wrote: "I have told in my book a tale of Jewish poverty in one ghetto, that of New York. The same story can be of a hundred other ghettoes scattered all over the world.[91] In the 1935 edition of his book, Michale Gold added, "Jews have lived for centuries in a universal ghetto".

Michael Gold's narrative conducts the reader through the rediscovery of thousands of other characters who, like the poor Jews of New York, rebuilt their lives in the Americas. Those are journeys that, for example, take us back to the life story of Jacob Gorender (1923–2013), a communist, a Jew, the son of Russian immigrants, who was born in Salvador (Bahia, Brazil). In an interview published in the magazine *Teoria e Debate*, Gorender tells that he was born into a very poor Jewish family, in the same category of those families described in Michael Gold's *Jews Without Money*. This is what Gorender said:

> My parents came from the former Russian Empire. My father, from Ukraine. My mother from Bessarabia. My father lived in Odessa for some time, where he witnessed the exceptional events of 1905. I was at the harbor when the battleship *Potemkin* was anchored there. That same year, he fought with Russian revolutionaries against the reactionary factions who tried to massacre the Jews. Then, with the failure of the 1905 Revolution, with the *pogroms* and all the terrible repression that ensued, he joined the great Jewish wave that left Russia. Nathan Gorender finally

---

91 Michael Gold, *Jews Without Money*, New York, Horace Liveright, 1930.

21. Fips, pseudonym of Philipp Rupprecht. Colored caricature "Do you know him?", Germany, 1933–1939. United States Holocaust Memorial Museum, courtesy Salo Klüger. ID Collection: 1992.66.1. Available at: https://collections.ushmm.org/search/catalog/pa1126743. Access: 08.08.2019.

arrived in Salvador. There, he settled in and married my mother, Ana, who arrived later. The five children and my parents belonged to that category of moneyless Jews described in a novel by Michael Gold, famous in the 1930s. We lived in tenements and sometimes we had serious difficulties in meeting even the most basic needs, such as food and clothing. That marked my mentality in formation.[92]

92 Paulo de Tarso Venceslau; Alipio Freire, interview "Jacob Gorender", in *Revista Teoria e Debate*, n. 11, July 1, 1990. Available at: http://www.teoriaedebate.org.br/materais/nacional/jacob-gorender#sthash.J9JPmPlg.dpuf. Retrieved: May 11, 2018.

22. Unidentified author. "Social Democracy in the 'mirror of the truth'". Caricature published in the Viennese magazine *Kikeriki*. Vienna, Austria, 1920. In the mirror is a Jew holding a money bag. Inside his jacket is an envelope marked "collections" and on the mirror is written "the noble race". Eduard Fuchs, *Die Juden in der Karikatur: ein Beitrag zur Kulturgeschichte*. Albert Langen, 1921. United States Holocaust Memorial Museum. Available at: https://collections.ushmm.org/search/catalog/pa1041752. Access: 08.08.2019.

The largest Jewish populations are concentrated in Israel which in 2019 counts approximately 6.4 million Israeli Jews of different ethnicities followed by the Jewish communities in the United States (5.7 million), France (475,000), Canada. (385,000), the United Kingdom (290,000), Russia (186,000), Germany (118,000), and Brazil (107,329).[93] Among those Jews, there are thousands of them who are in fact poor, some being even below the poverty line. Those numbers are ignored or totally unknown to the general population of any country where Jewish communities exist. Such inequalities persist as a consequence of economic crises, corruption and the absence of public policies aimed at the well-being of citizens. In the United States, according to Jacques Attali,

> [...] four-fifths of Jews now live in New York, Chicago and Los Angeles. Although a quarter of the American Jewish population still belongs to the working class, the German natives moved from the textile industry to the banks, leaving those other trades to more recent emigrants from the East, and then from the status of workers to that of lawyers, or from scrap dealers to traders; 60% now work in commerce and 17% in the professions.[94]

Situations such as the ones described were common in this 21st century and contributed to economic polarizations that impacted both Jews and non-Jews. Perhaps the case of the Jews

93 Data released in 2018 by the Bureau of Statistics, a state agency in cooperation with the Center for Contemporary Judaism Studies at the Hebrew University of Jerusalem. Total Jews in the world: 14.5 million; Joanne O'Brien; Martin Palme, *Atlas of Religions*, São Paulo, Publifolha, 2009.

94 Jacques Attali, *op. cit.*, pp. 497–498.

does not have as much visibility because the community itself, as far as possible, welcomes the needy, practicing *tsedakah* (from the Hebrew tsedek), a concept that integrates the Jewish tradition. *Tsedakah* is an act of generosity, justice and righteousness, and one that strikes at the economic and social differences strongly condemned in Judaism. Still, they are everywhere in the world. Let us refer to real-life situations: in the State of Israel, in February 2007, for example, there were 1,674,800 poor Jews, including 774,000 children, according to the National Security Report released by the Minister of Social Welfare. A year later, the poverty level fell to 1,630,400.[95]

Today, part of the Jewish population, especially in Latin America, faces difficult situations and poverty; some are malnourished despite the solidarity actions practiced by their communities. Most of poor Jews are young unemployed and former traders who went bankrupt, retired people, the elderly and the sick, who have no way to support themselves. They seek assistance from the synagogues and charities that traditionally welcome them since, to support and educate the poor and orphans, is among the three basic principles of life in the Talmud, as is charity and the practice of good deeds.

In São Paulo, for example, the needy Jewish community is cared for by the Israeli *Sociedade de Caridade TenYad*, a charitable society located in the district of Bom Retiro, which offers food, clothing and recreation, as well as day-care facilities to support mothers. Other institutions are UNIBES, *União Brasileiro-Israelita do Bem Estar Social* [Brazilian-Israelite Union

95 Vitor Carvalho Ferolla, "Existen judíos pobres", in *Israel Today News*, https://enfoqueisrael.blogspot.com.br/2012/06/existem-judeus-pobres-pobreza-apos-10.html?m=0. Retrieved: May 11, 2018.

for Social Welfare] created in 1976 after EZRA,[96] *Policlínicas*[97] and OFIDAS[98] merged. It is rooted in 1915, after the foundation of the *Sociedade Beneficente Amigos dos Pobres, EZRA* [Beneficent Society Friends of the Poor]. This institution was devoted to care for poor Jewish immigrants from the *schlechts* – Eastern European villages in Poland, Russia or Belarus – prior to World War II. In 1924, EZRA merged with *Sociedade Pró-Imigrante* [Pro-Immigrant Society] to become *Sociedade Beneficente Israelita EZRA* [Israelite Beneficent Society EZRA], with an extensive program of care for the needy.

Thus, through the history of immigration and institutions, it is possible to know details about the economic and social profile of Jewish immigrants who started to come to Brazil through the ports that were opened to *Friendly Nations* in 1810.

---

96 Associação de Socorro Ezra [Ezra Relief Association]: the oldest in São Paulo, was founded on May 25, 1916 by a group of Bessarabian Jews under the name of the "Sociedade Israelita Amiga dos Pobres" [Israeli Society Friends of the Poor]. From 1923, it began a program to protect immigrants, and on January 17, 1937 its field of action was expanded after the inauguration of a sanatorium for TB patients in São José dos Campos (SP).

97 Policlínica Linath Hatzedeck [Linath Hatzedeck Polyclinic]: it was founded on November 15, 1929 to provide medical assistance to sick immigrants, especially those who did not have a family or whose families were in Europe.

98 OFIDAS [Organização Feminina Israelita de Assistência Social]: The Israeli Women's Social Welfare Organization was founded on October 6, 1940, with the merger of the Sociedade Beneficente das Damas Israelitas [Israelite Ladies Benefit Society], Gota de Leite [Drop of Milk] and the Lar das Crianças Israelitas da Congregação Israelita Paulista [Home of the Israeli Children of the Israelite Paulista Congregation]. It was in charge of health, hygiene and medical and dental prophylaxis, pre-school education, language courses and professional orientation to immigrants and Nazi refugees.

In the immigration archives one can find that most of the pioneering Jews who came to Brazil were poor peasants from Eastern European villages who, facing many difficulties, managed to reconstitute their lives, helped by the communities that welcomed them. In Buenos Aires – which is today home to the first and most important Jewish community in Latin America, followed by Brazil – much of the social assistance to homeless Jews is provided by *Alianza Solidaria*, the *Tzedakah Foundation* and the *Emmanuel Temple*, which provides shelter, medicine, food and scholarships for Jewish children. Argentina's *Chabad Lubavitch*, for example, in 2002, was responsible for around 300 orphan Jewish children sent by the Court.

> A major study published by Bernardo Kliksberg, a UN Advisor and Chairman of the Commission on Human Development at the Latin American Jewish Congress, shows that in Argentina the process of impoverishment reached very high levels, with an estimated 50,000 Jews already living below the poverty line in 2002. Many of them belonged to the middle and lower sectors of the middle class that, since the 1990s, were shaken by the economic crisis that affected the country. Many were merchants who, with the increase in the number of shopping centers, large stores, supermarkets and the free entry of low price imports, were forced to file for bankruptcy.[99]

99 Bernardo Kliksberg, "A comunidade judaica da Argentina em perigo", in *Morashá*, ed. 36, March, 2002. Available at: http://www.morasha.com.br/judaismo-no-mundo/a-comunidade-judaica-da-argentina-em-perigo.html. Retrieved: May 11, 2018.

MYTH 5

The Jews Are Greedy

The myth says that all Jews are greedy, synonymous of stingy and mean in the popular jargon. The aimed sense is that Jews are perverse, evil, indifferent to the suffering of others, and that they are concerned exclusively with their own welfare. That is why – the antisemites explain – they are rich or, in the opposite sense, they live miserably, so as not to spend the profits they make at the expense of others. However, like all myths, the roots are much deeper and surpass the tone of mockery and inconsistent humor. Such accusations have served the political propaganda articulated in different places and moments in time to slander the Jews dispersed during the Diaspora.

Both the Catholic Church discourse and the political theories of the Renaissance have served to construct the myth that "all Jews are greedy and evil". Those are the sources that nourished the literature of the Elizabethan era produced, in this case, by Christopher Marlowe, William Shakespeare and Charles Dickens, among others.[100] Christopher Marlowe (1564–1593) created the character Barabbas in his work *The Jew of Malta,*

100 See the detailed analysis by Celi Barbosa dos Santos and Silvio Ruiz Paradiso, "A imagem do judeu na literatura britânica: Shylock, Barrabás e Gafin", in *Diálogos & Saberes,* Mandaguari, vol. 8, n. 1, 2012, pp. 213–231.

produced between 1589 and 1590, which strictly follows the methods proposed by Machiavelli: "no matter the means used to achieve the ends". In Marlowe's work, Barabbas, a wealthy Jewish merchant, is presented as a pervert, selfish, cold and unemotional man, whose profile was built from versions transmitted by the Catholic clergy, state authorities and the people. According to Silvio Ruiz Paradiso, a scholar of this literary production, Barabbas stands out as a diabolical, corrupt, Machiavellian and perverse being, "who, at the same time, devotes his life to the accumulation of gold, robbery, fornication etc."[101]

The talks by some of the characters created by Marlowe reveal how he lives and who Barabbas is. Ithamore, a slave of Barabbas, describes the Maltese Jew:

> He lives upon pickled grasshoppers and sauced mushrooms. [...] He never put on clean shirt since he was circumcised. [...] The hat he wears, Judas left under the elder when he hanged himself... [...] To undo a Jew is charity, and not sin.[102]

In Act V, Scene 2, author Marlowe gives voice to Barabbas, who confesses:

> This is the life we Jews are us'd to lead; and reason too, for Christians do the like.[103]

---

101 S. R. Paradiso. "Shakespeare: Anti-semita? A Imagem do Judeu em O Mercador de Veneza", in *Revista Cesumar, Ciências Humanas e Sociais Aplicadas*, Maringá, vol. 13, n. 1, 2008, p. 115.

102 Christopher Marlowe, *The Jew of Malta*. Edited by Rev. Alexander Dyce. Classic Literature Library, https://classic-literature.co.uk/christopher-marlowe-the-jew-of-malta/. Retrieved: May 24, 2018.

103 *Ibidem.*

The miserly profile of Barabbas reappears in Act II, Scene 3, during the purchase of a slave, when Barabbas describes the product he needs: "I must have one that's sickly, an't be but for sparing victuals". Sarcasm, hypocrisy, irony and lies are the elements applied to build the image of cruelty that Barabbas exhales, he, who despises the Other to the point of saying:

I learn'd in Florence how to kiss my hand,
Heave up my shoulders when they call me dog,
And duck as low as any bare-foot friar;
Hoping to see them starve upon a stall,
Or else be gather'd for in our synagogue,
That, when the offering-basin comes to me,
Even for charity I may spit into't.[104]

An array of value judgments exposed by Marlowe inspired one of Shakespeare's most complex comedies, *The Merchant of Venice* (1596), whose narrative takes up a set of antisemitic stereotypes inherited from the impositions sustained by the Catholic Church since the Middle Ages. Let us remember: during the Middle Ages it was considered a sin or a crime of heresy for Christians to lend money for profit, that is, to charge interests. At the end of the 16th century, such demands reached several Italian cities, including Venice, whose trade was concentrated in the circulation of exotic goods brought from overseas. The Jews were then able to lend money charging interest, an activity that strengthened the image of them as usurers and exploiters of other people (read Christians).

Thus, it is impossible to discuss *The Merchant of Venice* without analyzing antisemitism through the actions of the

104 *Ibidem.*

character Shylock, a Jewish usurer who is dehumanized by being compared to the figures of an "ordinary dog" or the devil. Money and usury reappear through the wicked and petty soul of this merchant who, in addition to being attacked by his "pagan race", bears the responsibility that "the Jews killed Christ". In the various presentations of the play, the character Shylock does not manage to break away from the threatening profile brought by the stigma of being a "filthy Jew" and "mean".

We take up here the aesthetics of cruelty presented on stage and applauded by the most diverse audiences: from the European aristocracy of the Modern Age to the German Aryan aristocracy of the Third Reich. Numerous are the records on *The Merchant of Venice* rehabilitated by the propaganda of Nazi Germany. As one might imagine, Goebbels did not miss the opportunity to use Shakespeare's text to instigate hatred against German Jews, who were also stigmatized in caricatures, photography and cinema. With some changes in the final part of the original text, the myth of the "mean and stingy Jew" was presented in about fifty different productions in Germany between 1933 and 1945. After that date, the disclosure of the genocidal atrocities committed by Nazis and collaborating countries has discouraged further presentations of the work.

This theme was brought to the 20th and 21st century in cinema, which took up, once again, *The Merchant of Venice*. In 1908 and 1912 two versions were performed in the United States; another one in Italy in 1910 (*Il Mercante di Venezia*). In 1923, the "Jewish merchant" was filmed in Germany (*Der Kaufman von Venedig*), with Werner Krauss in the role of Shylock, the same actor who, in 1943, would represent the *Jew Süss*, one of the antisemitic films produced by the Third Reich. In the 21st century, *The Merchant of Venice* reappeared in a film directed by Michael Radford, an East-Indian filmmaker living in London. In a homonymous rereading of William Shakespeare, after the Holocaust, the director encourages us to reflect on the ills of intolerance and the persistence of hatred against the Jews. The filmmaker reshapes the character Shylock – starring Al Pacino – who denounces the hypocrisy of Christian society that for centuries despised Jews and helped to strengthen the myth that they are avaricious men about to demand "their pound of flesh as the one who charges for centuries of persecution and segregation".[105]

This is a version that tries to drown out the myth that Jews are greedy and disgusting, which serves as a prophylaxis for the escalation of hatred. Cinema emerges then as a libel against anti-semitism which, rooted for centuries, reached its peak during the Holocaust. Al Pacino, in a magnificent representation, enriches the dignity of "being Jewish" in a dark and greyish Venice; it also presents Shylock as an observant man who respects the values of Judaism. According to Anna Stegh Camati, in her essay on this film by Michael Radford, the drop of blood that flows from the neck of the slaughtered animal, despite being a subtle image,

> [...] is one of the most significant in the film: it reminds us of the red wax used to seal the document that describes the terms of Shylock's loan to Antonio and reinforces the idea of bleeding, crucial to Shylock's defeat under Venice law. But the symbolism of bleeding transcends the work and is an allusion to another sacrifice, the Holocaust itself.[106]

---

105 Anna Stegh Camati, "O Mercador de Veneza, de Michael Radford: Adaptação, Historicização e Interpolação", en Anelise Reich Corseuil *et al.* (orgs.), *Ensaios de Literatura, Teatro e Cinema,* Florianópolis, Fundação Cultural Bades/Cultura Inglesa, 2013.

106 *Ibidem.*

This image – that of the greedy Jew – was constantly exploited by Nazi political propaganda. The intention was to spread antisemitism among the German people and the people of other countries. Film, photography and caricature have all served to portray Jews as subhuman beings and exploiters. Infiltrated as "rats" in the middle of the Aryan society, the Jews emerge as itinerant parasites, "consumed by sex, profit and money". That is the tone Fritz Hippler gave to his 1940 film *Der ewige Jude* [The Eternal Jew], whose stereotypical image was disseminated especially in public venues in Germany and Austria.

The caricature, for its critic disposition, pamphleteer nature and adversary essence, must be considered as a driving force behind antisemitic myths. In 1855, Charles Baudelaire published his text *De l'essence du rire…* [The Essence of Laughter].[107] Under this aspect – that of representation and as an artistic practice – I return back to the role of caricature, a singular genre capable of shaping minds and of expressing, at the same time, the collective mentality. It is precisely because of its perpetuity that the caricature was reestablished by antisemites in Nazi Germany and also in this 21st century, due to its ability to indoctrinate through laughter and the distortion of what is real.[108] It is with such a sense that I mention here the caricatures published by the Nazi weekly *Der Stürmer* (The Striker) which, due to its doctrinal role, left strong marks on the collective imagination. Published by Julius Streicher from

107 Charles Baudelaire, "De l'essence du rire et géneralement du comique dans les arts plastiques" (1855), in Henri Lemaitre (ed.), *Curiosités Esthétiques,* Paris, Garnier, 1986, p. 241.

108 Bertrand Tiller, *À la Charge! La Caricature en France de 1789 à 2000,* Paris, Les Éditions de l'Amateur, 2005, pp. 12–13. About the strength of myths in Nazi Germany, see François Perroux, *Les Mythes Hitlériens,* Paris, Librairie générale de droit et de jurisprudence, 1935.

23. Unidentified author. Image displayed at the entrance to the "Eternal Jew" Exhibition at the Vienna Railway Station, Austria, August 2, 1938. United States Holocaust Memorial Museum, courtesy of Morris Rosen. Available at: https://collections.ushmm.org/search/catalog/pa1129063. Access: 10.08.2019.

1923 until the end of World War II in 1945 – with brief interruptions – *Der Stürmer* was one of the main vehicles of the pamphleteering portrayal of Jews, although it also published pornographic, anticlerical and anti-capitalist texts.[109]

The myth of the miserly, child exploiter, cheater, rich, dirty and usurer man also circulated in children's books used by German schools as a pedagogy of hatred; among them, Ernst

109 After the war, Julius Streicher was tried and convicted by the Nuremberg Tribunal for crimes against humanity, incitement to hatred and genocidal proposals. The production of the newspaper *Der Stürmer* was presented as a main source of evidence of his antisemitism and virulence against various other ethnic and political groups.

„Wie die Giftpilze oft schwer von den guten Pilzen zu unterscheiden sind, so ist es oft sehr schwer, die Juden als Gauner und Verbrecher zu erkennen ..."

24. Fips, pseudonym of Philipp Rupprecht, author of the images illustrating the antisemitic German children's book *Der Giftpilz* [The Poison Mushroom] by Ernst Ludwig Hiemer. The caption reads: "Just as it is often very difficult to distinguish the poisonous from the edible mushrooms, it is often very difficult to recognize Jews as thieves and criminals...". Nuremberg [Bavaria], Germany, 1935. United States Holocaust Memorial Museum, ID: Collections: 1988.25.1. Available at: https://collections.ushmm.org/search/catalog/pa1069700. Access: 10.08.2019.

Ludwig Hiemer's *Der Giftpilz* (The Poisonous Mushroom), illustrated by German cartoonist Fips (pseudonym of Phillip Rupprecht). Published by Julius Streicher in 1938, with abundant color illustrations, this book left marks on children's minds with its virulent and antisemitic content. The images are in no way innocent and the messages are not subliminal: they lead children to evil attitudes, by reinforcing ethnic stereotypes:

> Jews are bad people. They are like poisonous mushrooms . . . Like poisonous mushrooms, they often cause misfortune . . . The Jew causes misery, sickness and death.[110]

Cartoons and Antisemitic Formulae

Cartoonists in the Americas "imported" from prints disseminated in the 18th and 19th centuries some basic models used to represent the greedy Jew. He is usually portrayed as a man with large, protuberant stomach and nose; he makes gestures that show the palms of his hand. According to John and Selma Appel, who analyzed comic books, the "German cartoonists added flat feet, curved legs and a taste for garlic . . .". In the same way, American cartoonists did not start from new images. There, the Jews appear:

> [. . .] according to European and Christian references, always unfavorable or hostile in relation to Jews who are intruders, christicides, strangers or representatives of the new and emerging capitalist society based on the impersonal exchange of goods and money.[111]

110 Ernst Hiemer, *Der Giftpilz,* Nuremberg, Stürmerverlag, 1938. German Propaganda Archive.

111 John Appel; Selma Appel, *Comics da Imigração na América,* trans. Sergio Roberto de Souza, São Paulo, Perspectiva, 1994, pp. 127–128.

Hundreds of antisemitic cartoons appeared from the 19th century onwards in the United States where, despite harboring one of the largest Jewish communities in the world has failed to protect Jews from unholy mockery. As we know, humor is a heinous weapon that reveals changes of mentality over the centuries. Freedom of speech, defended by democratic regimes, opened a channel for the proliferation of myths about Jews who remain a preferred target for sarcastic antisemitism. Loaded with ideologies, those cartoons incite hatred by lingering on cultural differences, ignorance and doubts that allow the persistence of stigma. Accused of enslaving their employees, Jews are presented as exploiters of female labor as well as sexual harassment. The illustration created by artist James Albert Wales (1852–1886) shows a line of jobseekers facing a lewd Jew, while three men behind a desk watch the selection process. Three vignettes complement the narrative and describe the degrading conditions for working women.

In Brazil, the figure of the avaricious Jew encountered its antisemitic interlocutors in literature and caricature at different historical times and, more specifically, during the period of the so-called *Estado Novo* [New State], presided by Getúlio Vargas (1937–1945). They reproduced the distinctive graphic formulae that depicted Jews with particular physical and dressing traits, used by cartoons that were usually displayed in European antisemitic prints. Some Brazilian illustrated magazines, such as *Careta, Cultura* and *Vamos Ler!*, appealed to the same symbolic elements used in Europe to portray the miserly Jew, the exploiter of peoples: bags of money, hats and black overalls, a gaze and claws that imitate birds of prey.[112]

112 Maria Luiza Tucci Carneiro, *O Anti-semitismo na Era Vargas: Fantasmas de uma geração,* 3. ed. São Paulo, Perspectiva, 2001, pp. 323–360.

25. James Albert Wales, *The Slaves of the Jews*, December 9, 1882. Chromolithography. Library of Congress Prints and Photographs Division, Washington, D.C.

By joining a stereotyped idea to a distorted image of a stingy and greedy Jew, the caricature reinforced, within the Brazilian population, attitudes of repulsion and contempt for the figure of the Jewish immigrant. Those forms of representation pleased the official discourse held by the repression agencies – such as the Ministry of Justice and Internal Affairs – and by the Brazilian Foreign Ministry, which considered Jews as "unassimilable, useless to society, destitute of scruples, without any aptitude for the agriculture, and also a factor for ethnic and religious disintegration".[113]

The silhouette of the Jew in the Brazilian cartoon resembles the features of the "German Jew" portrayed in posters and

113 Arguments cited by Hildebrando Accioly, Secretary General to Foreign Minister Oswaldo Aranha, Río de Janeiro, April 22, 1938, pp. 3–4. *Oficios Recebidos*, April 1938. AHI.

26. "O Faz Tudo" [The "Do It All"]. Caricature published in *Revista Careta*, October 1936 [cover]. Tucci Collection/ State of São Paulo/Brazil.

signs around Nazi Germany in the 1930s and 1940s. The same black overcoat, a long beard, portrayed in such a manner that expresses "an exploiter and a bad man" who holds in his hands a bag of money, gold coins and the world map, around which he throws his power. He is always a foreigner, a businessman, an exploiter of situations, a greedy individual and even a financier of wars, as highlighted by some American and German cartoons.[114]

A few years ago, on Brazilian television, the stigmatized image of the miserly Jew was incorporated by actor Marcos

114 *Revista Careta,* Rio de Janeiro, n. 1470, Aug. 1936, p. 39; n. 1460, June 1936; n. 439, Jan. 1936, p.31; n. 1449, Mar. 1936, p.34; n. 1467, Aug. 1936, p. 19; n. 1555, April 1938, cover; n. 1558, April 1938, cover; n. 1561, May 1938, cover; n. 1477, Oct. 1936, cover; n. 1580, Oct. 1938, p. 37. B.M.M.A.

Plonka (1939–2011), who played the character of the stingy Jew, Samuel Blaustein, in a TV show called *Escolinha do Professor Raymundo*, a comedy show directed by Chico Anísio at Globo TV channel. Many Brazilians remember the character's slogan that became the trademark of the "greedy Jew": "fazemos qualquer negócio" [we do any business]. It is important for the world's Jewish community to re-evaluate the appropriation of stigmatized expressions such as this one that negatively interfere with the collective imagination. Having in mind that Marcos Plonka was a Jew himself, making fun of this portrayal was like sticking an iron in his own chest. Today, in the face of the increasing power of media through social networks and the Internet, laughter can become a powerful instrument for manipulating minds: it seduces, and reinforces beliefs in absurdities and admiration for the grotesque. In short, laughter is part of life as well as the survival of myths: "Humor is always at the heels of doubt, that is, it is a double-edged sword".[115]

115 Georges Minois, *História do Riso e do Escárnio*, trad. Maria Elena O. Ortiz Assumpção, São Paulo, Editora Unesp, 2003, pp. 393, 632.

MYTH 6

The Jews Have No Homeland

The myth says that Jews have no homeland, which is why they would be walking eternally, having no territory or state, no rights or history. The expression "wandering Jew" is used to coin that identity aimed at demonstrating that this or that group (or individual) lives at the margins and symbolizes a danger to national security or established values. In short, any of those groups can be sinners, heretics, criminals, deranged, terrorists, imperialists, etc.

The expression that Jews "have no homeland" or that "they are eternal travelers" does not refer only to the past: over the centuries, it has been repeated and updated according to the interests of different social and political groups and has served to justify one or other ideology. The figure of the wandering Jew was rehabilitated under new masks, because the archetype helps to promote intolerant discourses that, adapted to the reality in which they circulate, feed hatred and violence not only against Jews, but also against Africans and other minorities. Considering that our minds are true recipients of mental projections, such images, by maintaining close plausibility with reality, adapt themselves and help to perpetuate the lie.

Between the 19th and 20th centuries, when the myth was transformed under the influence of modern antisemitism, the polymorphic figure of the wandering Jew resonated politically and culturally, and served to explain the constant dislocations and persecutions of Jews who were identified as the "people of the Diaspora".[116] According to an analysis by Galit Hansan-Rokem, a professor at the Hebrew University of Jerusalem, the proliferation of this legend, full of meanings, has also served Europeans who were interested in strengthening their identity as a people settled and rooted in one specific place. From this perspective, Jews became easy targets for accusations as they escaped the paradigm of a people established in one territory. Despite the existence of the State of Israel since 1948, they are still not devised within the idealized structure of a nation swtate, a concept that expresses the image of modern Europe, legitimized by a collective order and identity. This lack of frame makes them vulnerable to hatred since they would correspond to the idea of a "stranger without a homeland", an eternal stranger.[117]

In the 20th century, the image of the wandering Jew reappeared in the image of the "stateless passenger", expelled and dehumanized by German National-Socialism. He no longer resembled the medieval Christian figure, but still was a symbol of the uprooted and the depiction of the Other. This new attire also serves the anti-Zionists who, by means of repetition, insist that Jews have no right to return to their homeland (former Palestine) or even to have a homeland. Such statements have served to call into question the legitimacy of the State of Israel, demonstrating that those simplistic assessments overshadow the

---

116 Galit Hansan-Rokem, in *Le Juif Errant est Revenu*. Commissaire de l'exposition Laurence Sigal-Klasbald, Musée d'Art et d'Histoire du Judaïsme, 2001; Bernadette Sauvaget, "Le Juif Errant est Revenu", in *La Vie*, n. 2931, Oct. 31, 2001.

117 Zigmunt Bauman, *Life in Fragments: Essays in Postmodern Morality*, Oxford, Blackwell, 1995.

interpretation of facts with Manichean values. In this context – that of unreasonableness – antisemitism has found a fertile ground to proliferate, damaging the peace negotiations in the Middle East as well as the image of the State of Israel and of Jews in the contemporary world.

Actually, as with every myth, the Wandering Jew is a literary construction that, over the centuries, has received multiple versions, that adds to the fabrication "the Jews killed Christ". It has spanned centuries and, between the 13th and 21st centuries, has also brought together elements for the elaboration of new concepts that promote intolerance and boundless hatred. The "wandering Jew", the "uprooted man", the "banished", the "stateless" and "citizen of the world" are all archetypes that coexist in the collective imaginary and have inspired novels, poems, songs, films, popular literature, drama, pamphlets, drawings, cartoons, sculptures, paintings and acts of violence.

Images of the Wandering Jew

From the assertion that Jews do not have a homeland, one can identify several characters whose images have in common the belief that Jews are condemned to wander around the world for having denied water to Jesus and for not allowing him to rest on his way to the Calvary. According to the Gospels, Jesus – carrying the cross on his back and being lashed by the Roman guards – stood before an old Jew who asked for water; he said no, pushed Jesus and ordered him to keep walking. Jesus answered, "I will go on, but you will wait until I return." And he continued his walk to Golgotha.

The image of the old Jew, who denied water to Jesus, has gotten different names along the centuries, depending on the country where the story is told: Isaac Laquedem of the tribe of

Levi, Cataphytus or Cataphithite, Buttadeu, John Hope-in-God, Melmoth, Mattathias, Jerusalemin Suutari, Ahasuerus, Ahasvero and Assuerus (Hebrew transcription of the name of the Persian King Xerxes). Regardless of its various names, this character, according to the legend, was victim of a divine curse, which condemned him to walk forever: an eternal journey that would last until the day of the Last Judgment when, according to the Scriptures, Jesus will return to Earth.

According to some scholars, such as Charles Schoebel [1813–1888] and Gaston Paris [1839–1903],[118] the wandering Jew is Cain who, according to the Bible, killed Abel and, after the crime, became a fugitive and a wanderer on earth: Then the Lord put a mark on Cain so that no one who found him would kill him. So Cain went out from the Lord's presence and lived in the land of Nod, east of Eden.[119]

Among the various folk tales collected in the Qr'an, one of them deals with another tireless traveler, a Samaritan, cursed by Moses for having made the golden calf. He picked up his tents and, from that time, he roams the world like a wild beast:

> [...] a wild beast, from one end of the world to the other. Everyone flees and purifies the ground their feet have trodden on, and when he approaches a man himself, he cries constantly, "Do not touch me!". He warns his companions to stay away from him, for, according to later legends, contact brings them fever. His perpetual move-

118 Charles Schoebel, *La Légende du Juif Errant*, Paris, 1877; Gaston Paris, *Le Juif Errant. Première Étude*. http://www.biblisem.net/etudes/parislje.htm. Retrieved: June 1, 2018.

119 Genesis 4:1–16, *The Bible*. New International Version. Available at: https://www.biblegateway.com/passage/?search=Genesis+4%3A1-16&version=NIV. Retrieved: May 28, 2018.

> ment made him give the name of Kharaïti, or "Turner". Arab sailors transformed the "old Jew" into a sea monster with a human face, with a white beard that sometimes appears at dusk on the surface of the waves.[120]

This legend, according to Gaston Paris, coincidentally, is very similar to the legends that gather around the memory of the Passion of Christ. In his opinion, popular imagination added new episodes to the stories of the Gospels involving Judas, Pilate, the two thieves, Joseph of Arimathea, Berenice (Veronica), Longino the blind man, among others. The sum of these myths served the theological Christian anti-Judaism as a sort of "witness" to strengthen faith in Jesus Christ and bring "truth" to the facts narrated in the Gospels.[121] Innumerable mental configurations result from those multiple narratives that, even today, are projected in Europe, especially during the Holy Week, when Catholics remember the Passion of Christ. Such tensions also strengthen the relation with the fact that Jews do not recognize the Messiah in Christ.

Paths Travelled by the Wandering Jew

Back to the 13th century, we identify one of the first versions of the legend of the wandering Jew who, according to oral tradition, had been told by an archbishop of Great Armenia during his visit to the monastery of Saint-Alban. This clergyman said that he had had lunch with Joseph (or Cartaphilus), the porter

---

120 *El Corán*, XX, v.89 and subsequently, p. 94; Schoebel, p. 57, cited by Gastón de Bruno Paulin Paris, *Légendes du Moyen Âge*, Paris, Hachette, 1912.

121 Gastón de Bruno Paulin Paris, *op. cit.*

of the praetorium, who, for having beaten Jesus, was condemned to await the return of the Lord. Every hundred years Joseph fell into lethargy, recovering the physical appearance of a 30-year-old man, his age at the time of Christ's martyrdom on the way to the Calvary.

The legend, which was constantly reiterated, continued its metamorphosis until 1233, when a chronicler from Bologna wrote that Emperor Frederick II had heard from a pilgrim that in Armenia there was a Jew condemned by Our Lord Jesus Christ to be an eternal wanderer. In 1228, Roger de Wendover, an English historian, claimed that Joseph confessed to having served Pontius Pilate, a version that was restated in the *Chronique Rimée* by Philippe Mousket, Bishop of Tournai, around 1243. Years later, in 1252, the Benedictine Monk and Archbishop Matthew Paris quoted the same fact in his illustrated manuscript *Chronica Majora* 1240–1251, where he portrays the encounter of the wandering Jew with Christ on his way to the Calvary. There are those who argue that, for having been employed by Pilate, Cataphitus was Roman and not Jewish. Among them, the already mentioned medievalist Gaston de Bruno Paulin Paris (1839–1903), in the several editions of his *Légendes du Moyen Age* (1902, 1903, 1912, 1972).[122]

The encounters with the wandering Jew continued to occur, assisted by the dynamics of the myth that assumed modern forms from a German pamphlet disseminated throughout several European countries, in many languages: *Kurtze Beschreibung und Erzählung von einen Juden mit Namen Ahasuerus* [Short description and narration from a Jew named Ahasuerus], from June 9th, 1564. In this chronicle, the author (anonymous) insisted on

122 Legend narrated at http://cronicasdeasgardh.blogspot.com.br/2006/05/o-judeu-errante.html. Retrieved: June 1, 2018.

having seen the wandering Jew in Schleswig and described him as "a tall, long-haired man, with the soles of his feet tanned and speaking good Castilian for having lived in Madrid". And what's more, he had a wife and children who had been with him for a long time. His sin: "to have offended the son of God"; his punishment: "to walk forever". On June 29, 1564, Paul von Eitzen, a Doctor of Theology and the Bishop of Schleswig, claimed to have found the wandering Jew in Hamburg in 1542. Creativity did not stop here: in 1575, the wandering Jew was seen again in Spain and France (in Strasbourg and Beauvais), and inspired artistic productions that shaped and granted the story an apparent veracity.

According to historian Marcello Massenzio, the stereotypical figure named Ahasuerus (Aasvero, Ahsvero or Assuero, the shoemaker from Jerusalem) emerged in 1602; its matrix comes from the image reproduced in the *Chronicle Majora*, by Matthew Paris. It was replicated in an apocryphal pamphlet entitled *Kurtze Beschreibung und Erzählung von einem Juden mit Namen Ahasuerus* [A Brief Account of a Jew of Name Ahasuerus], printed in Leiden (Germany), in 1602, by a certain Christoff Crutzer, which might be a pseudonym. In 1609, another pamphlet was published in Bordeaux (France) – *Discours du Véritable Juif Errant* [Discourses of the True Wandering Jew] – translated from the German pamphlet *Kurze Beschreibung und Erzählung,* from 1564. Chrysostomus Dudulaeus (a pseudonym) published the same legend with the title of *Wunderbarlicher Bericht* [Wonderful Report]. It was not by chance that the myth of the wandering Jew resonated greatly in Germany and France, traditionally antisemitic nations.

Particularly in France during the Napoleonic era, the figure of the wandering Jew became an obsession, without losing the moral essence of the medieval Christian legend: in a few decades, approximately two million popular engravings proliferated; over the centuries, they were adapted in ways that contributed to haunt the collective imagination. It also attracted feuilleton creators, among them, the French Joseph Marie Eugène Sue (1804–1857), author of the first novel-feuilleton *Le Juif Errant* [The Wandering Jew] (1844–1845), inspired by an image created by Gustave Doré (1832–1883).[123] Italian author Umberto Eco, in his historical novel *The Prague Cemetery*[124] demonstrates how *The Protocols of the Elders of Zion,* which denounced an alleged Jewish plot to dominate the world, originated from distorted versions of scenes from Eugène Sue's *The Wandering Jew,* and Alexandre Dumas's *Joseph Balsamo*.

In 1834, the myth of Ahasuerus was modernized with the poem in prose by Edgard Guinet (1803–1875), a controversial historian who, in his text, delivers the verdict that God gave Christ to the human race; in turn, a single man would be cursed: the Jew, condemned to walk eternally. In 1846, Guinet was expelled from the *Collège de France* for his criticism of the Roman Catholic Church, for exalting the revolution, for supporting the oppressed nationalities of France, and for defending the theory that "religion is a determinant force in

123 Annie Renonciat, *La Vie et l'Oeuvre de Gustave Doré,* Paris, ACR Editions, 1983 (343 illustrations); Helio Lopes, *Letras de Minas e Outros Ensaios,* São Paulo, Edusp, 1997; Jerusa Pires Ferreira, "O Judeu Errante: A Materialidade da Lenda", in *Revista Olhar,* Universidade Federal de São Carlos, ano 2, n. 3, 2000, http://www.olhar.ufscar.br/index.php/olhar/article/viewFile/21/20 . Retrieved: June 1, 2018.

124 Umberto Eco, *The Prague Cemetery,* Boston, Houghton Mifflin Harcourt, 2011.

27. Gustave Doré, "The Wandering Eternal Jew". France, 1852. Reprinted in an antisemitic publication by Eduard Fuchs, *Die Juden in der Karikatur: ein Beitrag zur Kulturgeschichte*, Albert Langen, 1921. Copyright: United States Holocaust Memorial Museum. Available at: https://collections.ushmm.org/search/catalog/pa1041714. Access, 10.08.2019.

28. Charles François Pinot (1917–1979), *Le Vrai Portrait by Juif-Errant* [The True Portrait of the Wandering Jew], Engraving, Epinal, Vosges, France, c. 1857. Musée d'art et d'histoire du Judaïsme. Paris, France [Inv. 94.23.003]. Available at: https://www.mahj.org/en/decouvrir-collections-betsalel/le-vrai-portrait-du-juif-errant-52482. Access: 10.08.2019.

29. Text and music *Véritable Complainte du Juif-Errant (Imagerie d'Épinal)*, n. 5bis, 238 × 260mm, Feuilleton published in France, circa 1880, Pellerin & Cie. Tucci Collection/State of São Paulo/Brazil.

society".[125] In 1857, Charles François Pinot (1917–1979) created another version for the figure of the Wandering Jew, the same cobbler who in Jerusalem had insulted Christ and refused to help him carry the cross. In this print, old Ahasveru, in colorful clothes, runs away scared from the curse symbolized by a cross and a serpent at his feet.

In the 20th century, the expression "wandering Jew" reached new dimensions, and was also used to discriminate against other minorities who, as immigrants or "barbarians", were considered as individuals on the fringes of society. As an expression of this racist interpretation are the pamphlets created by King Wachirawut of Siam (1910–1925), who applied antisemitic stereotypes to Chinese merchants identified as enemies of the kingdom. The titles on the texts indicate their purpose: *The Jews of the Orient* (1914) and *Clogs on Our Wheels* (1915). After studying in England, Wachirawut became a follower of European nationalism, which, in the 20th century, was directly linked to racist theories applied to state projects, such as was the case in Germany (National Socialism) and Italy (Fascism).[126]

In the United States, the image of the wandering Jew acquired a political bias and served to illustrate the path taken by Paul Kruger (1825–1905), who, at that time, was exiled in Europe. After serving four terms as the president of the South African Republic (or Transvaal Republic), Kruger left his country amidst the Second Boer War, which began on October 11th, 1899. He escaped on board the battleship *Der Gelderland*,

---

125 Edgard Guinet, *Ahasvérus*, Paris, Revue de Deux Mondes, 1834; Bibliothèque Nationale de France. Available at: http://gallica.bnf.fr/ark:/12148/bpt6k5529161k.texteImage. Retrieved: June 1, 2018.

126 Benedict Anderson, *Imagined Communities: Reflections on the Origin and Spread of Nationalism,* New York, Verso Books, 2006.

30. François Georgin, *Le Juif-Errant (Imagerie d'Épinal)*. Engraving. Perhinderion I, 1896. Spencer Museum of Art. Purchase; The Letha Churchill Walker Memorial Art Fund, 1997.

sent by Queen Wilhelmina of the Netherlands, which travelled across Marseilles and the Netherlands to Clarens in Switzerland. There, he died on July 14th, 1904. The image of the "Wandering Paul Kruger" was depicted in a chromolithography by artist Udo J. Keppler (1872–1956), published by Puck – a pioneering weekly magazine of graphic humor and political satire – on January 9th, 1901. The composition is intriguing: in the foreground it depicts a man with physiognomic features that are different from the traditional caricature of the wandering Jew.

But, like Gustave Doré's (1852) *Wandering Jew*, Kruger walks like a fugitive in disarranged clothing and supports himself with a cane. He leaves behind some soldiers who expel him with a gesture of repulse. In the sky, dark clouds express the dark times experienced by Kruger in exile.[127]

In Germany, the myth of the Wandering Jew was used by the ideologues of National Socialism. The Reich propaganda media exploited this character widely, relying on antisemitic pamphlets produced since the 17th century. In the poster of the exhibition *Der ewige Jude* (The Eternal Jew), exhibited in Munich on November 8th, 1937, the figure emerges with a new look, detached from the classic images. He is no longer a wanderer but a still figure, with a not very long beard, wearing black clothes and a hat. Instead of his traditional walking stick, he holds a whip and, under his arm, he brings a map of the USSR marked with the symbol of the hammer and sickle. In the palm of his outstretched hand he holds a handful of coins, an analogy to the Jew's greedy character. Overall, his silhouette is frightening and causes a certain repulsion towards a figure that represents not only the dangerous Jew, but also Marxists, usurers and slavers.[128]

This type of image was aimed at strengthening the idea of malignancy attributed to Jews who represented a degenerate race and had lost their citizenship rights. Once stateless, they were excluded from state protection as enemies of the German people. As Jews, they carried the mark of degeneration and as outcasts, according to those ideologues, should be extermi-

---

127 Prescott Holmes, *The Life Story of the President of the Transvaal*, Philadelphia, Henry Altemus.

128 Poster of the exhibition *Der Ewige Jude* (The Eternal Jew), Munich, November 8, 1937.

31. Udo Keppler, "The Wandering Jew". Chromolithography, *Puck*, v. 48, no. 1244, January 9, 1901. Ills. In AP101.P7 1901, Library of Congress Prints and Photographs Division, Washington, D.C.

nated, with no need to wait for the Last Judgment, as the legend of the wanderer Jew proclaimed. The image of Jesus Christ on the way to the Calvary disappears from the narrative, as does any other reference to pictures of the Passion, based on the Gospels. The future of the Jews – extermination – had already been foreseen by Adolf Hitler in *Mein Kampf* [My Struggle], the bible of National Socialists. This genocidal solution was expressed in the film *Der ewige Jude,* directed by Fritz Hippler and filmed after the German invasion of Poland, in September 1939. It premiered on November 29, 1940 for a special audience made up of representatives of the German Arts, Sciences and Armed Forces (the *Wehrmacht*). Commissioned by Goebbels, the film shows "authentic scenes made in Polish ghettos" showing what Jews were like "before hiding under the mask of civilized Europeans". Those images are then replaced by rats who, in an analogy with the Jews, "disseminate destruction around them, spoiling food and property"; "they obtain gains from the sickness of the people"; "they spread diseases, the plague, leprosy, typhoid fever, cholera and dysentery"; "The rootless Jew has no organs".[129] The film director, Fritz Hippler, was convicted by the U.S. Military Court after the war, along with cartoonist Philipp Ruprecht, from the daily *Der Stürmer,* Otto Dietrich and Max Amann, both from the Reich's press.

Despite the atrocities committed by the Nazis during the Holocaust, antisemitic myths continue to multiply throughout the world, maintaining the prominence of texts and images made about the undesirable Jew. The contemporary world continues to be a "host" of the myth of the Wandering Jew,

---

129 *Der ewige Jude, Ein dokumentarischer Film der D.F.G. Musik,* Franz R. Friedl, 1940.

32. "The Wandering Jew". From the antisemitic German children's book, "Trau Keinem Fuchs . . .", by Elvira Bauer – *Der Stürmer*. Germany, 1936. Caption: "Trust no fox in the green meadow and no Jew on his oath". United States Holocaust Memorial Museum. Available at: https://collections.ushmm.org/search/catalog/pa1069747. Access: 10.08.2019.

favored by persistent questions about the rights of the Jewish people to the territories of ancient Palestine and the dispersion of Jewish communities across all continents, a setting for incursions into the world of fiction. Once again, in Umberto Eco's words, one has to admit that:

> [...] in order to impress ourselves, to get disturbed, frightened or even moved, even with the most impossible of worlds, we count on our knowledge of the real world.[130]

Brazil, Host of the Myth

The legend of the Wandering Jew has always been present in Brazil and is subtly nourished by an intolerant and antisemitic mentality that has persisted since the 16th century. Inspired by European models, several pamphlets were produced or translated between 1844 and 1900 in Brazil, which confirms the taste for this kind of literature. The text *Le Juif Errant* (The Wandering Jew), by Eugène Sue (1804–1857), for example, was published in the newspaper *Diário do Rio de Janeiro*, on October 29th, 1844; it was transcribed from the newspaper *A Restauração*, from Lisbon, Portugal. On December 5, 1845, the same newspaper announced the sale of Sue's "fantastic Wandering Jew, in 5 volumes, for 2$rs". The book was launched in Brazil in June 1845, amidst great furor, despite criticisms by

130 Umberto Eco, *Seis Passeios pelos Bosques da Ficção . . . , op. cit.*, p. 89; Cristiane Soares Fernandes, "Resenha: Análise dos conceitos fundamentais apresentados no Cap. 4 – Bosques Possíveis", from the book "Seis Passeios pelos Bosques da Ficção", by Umberto Eco. http://pt.scribd.com/doc/23998943/Analise-do-livro-Seis-Passeios-pelos-Bosques-da-Ficçao-Umberto-Eco. Retrieved: June 1, 2018.

Father Lopes Gama, who considered it a "moralizing and scathing pamphlet"[131].

A play, based on the novel, was soon taken to the stage at *Teatro Lírico* in Rio de Janeiro, and $10,000 *contos de réis*[132] were spent to stage the drama. As in Europe, the figure of Ahasuerus – sometimes an immortal pilgrim, sometimes an oppressor of Jesus – was reproduced and multiplied in music sheets, postcards, poems, engravings and paintings. Some voices, identified with the life of the uprooted, took up again the accursed theme of the wandering Jew to compose their texts and/or autobiographies. Indignant poems, such as those by Castro Alves (1847–1871) and Luis Nicolau Fagundes Varela (1841–1875), reinterpreted the figure of the wandering Jew, an archetype that inspired many of their melodramas. Castro Alves, in *Ahasuerus e o Gênio* [Ahasuerus and the Genius], used the figure of the "miserable Jew who stamped on his forehead the mark of the atrocious", "the eternal traveler of the eternal path…". As stated by Castro Alves, the poet of slaves, Genius was like Ahasuerus, "…alone/Marching, marching on his way/With no end".[133]

As a demonstration against the universal rejection experienced by Black slaves and Jews, Castro Alves reinterpreted the drama of the wandering Jew – who was "cursed", just like him,

131 *Diário do Rio de Janeiro,* Dec. 5, 1845, cited by Egon y Frieda Wolff, *Os Judeus do Brasil Imperial,* São Paulo, Centro de Estudos Judaicos/FFLCH-USP, 1975. For more details about the wandering Jew see Maria Luiza Tucci Carneiro, *O Veneno da Serpente, op. cit.,* pp. 31–45.

132 A currency used in Brazil in the 18th century. As a reference we have that the price of a six-years old Black slave was 800 *contos de réis.*

133 Cited by Alfredo Bosi, *Brazil and the Dialectic of Colonization.* Translated by Robert Patrick Newcomb. Chicago, University of Illinois Press, 2015, p. 218.

an irreverent poet – in *Vozes da África* [Voices of Africa] (1866). Alves explains the stigmatization of blacks based on the myth of racial condemnation, whose historical fate was irreversible. Thus, the poet from Bahia sings, in verses, the drama of the Blacks who, for millennia, and like the Jews, were condemned to pay for their sins:

Vi a ciência desertar do Egito
Vi meu povo seguir – Judeu maldito –
Trilho de perdição
Depois vi minha prole desgraçada
Pelas graças d'Europa – arrebatada –
Amestrado falcão![134]

Fagundes Varela, in some of his poems *Noturnas* [Nocturnals], refers to the martyrdom and pains of the wandering Jew: "On whose wind-burned face, a fiery tongue was written in flame!![135] The subject is retaken in *Mocidade e Morte* [Youth and Death] in which Ahasuerus symbolizes the figure of the accursed, a reference analyzed by Jerusa Pires Ferreira in her essay *O Judeu Errante: A Materialidade da Lenda* [The Wandering Jew: the Materiality of the Legend].[136]

In the 1850s, Eugène Sue's *The Wandering Jew* was

134 "I saw learning abandoning Egypt.../I saw my people follow -damned Jew-/The road to perdition./Then I saw my disgraced tribe/Snatched by the jaws of Europe/ trained falcon!...". Castro Alves, *Voices from Africa*, June 1, 1886. Cited by Alfredo Bosi, *op. cit.*, p. 216.

135 Cited by Alfredo Bosi, *op. cit.*, p. 219.

136 Jerusa Pires Ferreira. "O Judeu Errante. A Materialidade da Lenda". In, *Revista Olhar*, Ano 2, N. 3, June 2000. Available at: http://www.olhar.ufscar.br/index.php/olhar/article/viewFile/21/20. Retrieved: June 1, 2018.

included in the list of books revered by the Brazilian *intelligentsia,* which equated this text to those by Alexandre Dumas and Victor Hugo. As an author of *feuilletons,* Sue – despite his references to ugliness, evil, crime, darkness and horror – was read and acclaimed by graduates from the Law Schools of São Paulo and Rio de Janeiro States. The Viscount of Taunay[137] recorded in 1852, that he got from his uncle Beaurepaire's library in the district of Engenho Novo, Rio de Janeiro, "eight thick volumes" of *The Wandering Jew,* published in Brussels. In short: "He devoured them endlessly!" Brito Broca[138] quoted Eugène Sue among the preferred authors of a character from one of his writings, Viscount of Nogueira Gama's (1855).[139]

One thing is certain: wherever the "wandering Jew" walked, he became uncomfortable company. This is how the Brazilian poet Carlos Drummond de Andrade (1902–1987) described him in one of his works published in 1968. Analyzed by author Kênia Maria de Almeida Pereira, this poem reached

---

137 Viscount of Taunay or Alfredo Maria Adriano d'Escragnolle Taunay (1843–1899), Brazilian, from an aristocratic family. A great admirer of D. Pedro II He was a writer, a military and a politician during the period called in Brazil, the empire. His grandfather, painter Nicolas Antoine Taunay, arrived in Brazil with the French Mission in 1816.

138 José Brito Broca (1903–1961), Brazilian, a literary critic and historian. From 1924 he started to write chronicles for several newspapers in São Paulo under the pseudonyms "Lauro Rosas" and "Alceste". In the late 1930s, he moved from São Paulo to Rio de Janeiro, where he began to work at the DIP – Department of Press and Propaganda, a censorship organ founded by the *Estado Novo.* He also worked as an editor at the publisher house *Livraria José Olympio* and the newspaper *A Gazeta.*

139 Cited by Marlyse Meyer, *Folhetim, uma História,* São Paulo, Companhia das Letras, 1996, p. 286.

another dimension, and entered the field of psychology. By means of his verses Drummond recovers his fears as a child born and raised in Itabira (Minas Gerais). Intrigued by the story of this dangerous man who "walks and walks and treads on my sleep", Drummond confesses that he never fell asleep without thinking of the Wandering Jew. He heard the footsteps of that man dressed in black resounding in his bedroom: "... under the bed, in the wardrobe drawer, at the doorstep of my sleep!" Distressed, he asks questions: Does the Wandering Jew have a bed? Does he eat in the air? Does he leave footprints? What is his voice like? Like Drummond, many other children suffered sleepless nights and covered their heads with their sheets to avoid facing the "bearded man who wandered through the dark streets of small towns, cursing families and stealing from naughty children".[140] This figure leads us to the stigmatized image of the gypsy who, like the Jew, also carries the stigma of the wanderer.

In the 1930s, Drummond most likely crossed paths with Eugène Sue's *Le Juif Errant,* published in Brazil by Paulista, a publishing house from São Paulo state.[141] In April 1934, the text was advertised in the catalogue (n. 1) published by *A Sementeira,* and was recommended along other titles authored by names such as Fyodor Dostoyevsky, Maxim Gorky and Victor Hugo.[142]

140 Kenia Maria de Almeida Pereira, "O Judeu Errante nas Minas Gerais: Carlos Drummond de Andrade em Busca de Aventuras", in *Arquivo Maaravi: Revista Digital de Estudos Judaicos da UFMG,* Belo Horizonte, vol. 7, n. 13, Oct. 2013

141 Eugène Sue, *O Judeu Errante,* São Paulo, Editorial Paulista, s.d. Biblioteca Mindlin/USP.

142 *Catálogo de Propaganda de Livros* (n. 1), from *A Sementeira,* confiscated and annexed to *Pront. n.* 581, Delegacia Regional de Polícia de Jundiaí, vol. I, Fundo Deops/SP.

At the same time, the French edition of *Le Juif Errant*, illustrated by Gavarni, was published in four volumes.

The Wanderer in Cordel Literature

The dissemination of the legend of the wandering Jew can be confirmed by its presence in *cordel* booklets, one of the most important forms of record in Brazilian popular culture. The *cordel* brochures – which are the *"newspapers" of those who do not read newspapers on the Brazilian northeast coast* – have a mythical force that take on the form of a plague, death or betrayal.[143] This is a sign that the narrative constructed by the authors of *cordel* literature created matrices that populate the imaginary and promote a particular worldview. According to Lise Andriès, this form of literature must be seen as "a system of interpretation of the magical and religious world".[144]

For this reason, scholars devoted to the study of racism and particularly antisemitism, should not detract from those specifications. Popular authors seek to concentrate their stories on easily recognizable figures, such as Jesus Christ, the Jew, the Black, the Gypsy, the immigrant, etc., as well as on places such as Jerusalem, Rome or Turkey. Their goal, to imprint credibility to their stories.

Among *cordel* booklets one must mention *A Vida do Judeu Errante* [The Life of the Wandering Jew], by Manoel Apolinário Pereira, who decided to write a treatise on the life of this man who "ignored God and disobeyed all His orders". Inspired by

143 Ricardo Noblat, "Fatos e Fotos e Manchete", cited by Mark J. Curran, *História do Brasil em Cordel,* São Paulo, Edusp, 2001, pp. 24–25.

144 Lise Andriès. *Le Grand Livre des Secrets – Le Colportage en France aux 17e et 18e siècles,* Paris, Éditions Imago, 1994, p. 17.

Enrique Pérez Escrich's novel *The Martyr of Golgotha: A Picture of Oriental Tradition*, the author narrates the story of Samuel Belibeth (Ahasuerus), a mercenary soldier who, in his wandering, travelled several nations.[145]

The monstrous profile of Samuel Belibeth is constructed by the singer, verse by verse, who describes him as an ugly, very tall and strong man, with a frightening voice. Belibeth "killed people, he did not believe in saints and his God was the sword". After returning to Jerusalem, this man got married and, in order to support his family, he devoted himself to trade, "out of obligation". His wife died ten months after giving birth to a child who, according to the author, was "in the hands of that Jew who could not even care for his own mother who was paralyzed, deaf and mute". To make a connection with the trajectory of Jesus Christ, the author calls Belibeth a charlatan who, laughing out loud, suggested to his sister-in-law Seraphia that "he should have fun with the gestures that the Son of God made on the cross".

The author continues, giving an accusing tone to the narrative by involving Belibeth in the crucifixion of Christ: "He accused Jesus in the most aggravating way, dragged him to the stand and slapped him on the back while the people laughed out loud". We can note that, for Samuel Belibeth, Jesus the Nazarene was a "false prophet", "a profaner of the lights of the empire", "a false lord" and "an unhappy sorcerer" who coveted the throne of Emperor Tiberius. During Jesus' journey to the Calvary, Belibeth denied him water and rest; he also accused Jesus of being "a false son of God". Jesus would have told Samuel that, as a punishment, Belibeth would become immortal; but his immortality would not bring him happiness: he would walk unceasingly, wandering around the world until the last day.

145 Cited by Jerusa Pires Ferreira, *op. cit.*

33. Unidentified author, "The Wandering Jew". Cartoon from the *Shanghai Evening Post* portraying the plight of Jewish refugees in Asia. Shanghai, [Kiangsu] China, February 4, 1941. United States Holocaust Memorial Museum, courtesy of Eric Goldstaub. Available at: https://collections.ushmm.org/search/catalog/pa1083443. Access: 10.08.2019.

Hence the phrase that supports the errant Jew's sentence: "Walk, walk, Belibeth – up to eternity?"[146]

On *A Vida do Judeu Errante* [The Life of the Wanderer Jew], one can see that the image that is constructed in the text moves between animalesque and human forms, both cursed by the book's author. The emphasis is on the idea of predestination: that a doomed man is condemned to flee and escape – from nation to nation – in order to fulfill his difficult mission. The use of qualifying adjectives at the end of each *stanza* stigmatizes the character, who carries the stain of being "filthy and cursed by God". In the end, the author warns: if the wandering Jew tries to come to Brazil – "a brilliant land where people are rebellious… he will bring it to boil".[147] Once again, the image of the wandering Jew corresponds to the figure of a stateless Jew, a homeless wanderer who was expelled from Germany by the Nazis. Here we are placed before a refurbishing of the myth that, when crossed with another myth (the one that the Jews killed Christ), gets a popular version that is easily understood by semi-illiterate Brazilian citizens. In other words, there are multiple versions that, guided by codes that govern the elaboration of the literary text, make the reader hate that Jew. Thus, between 1933 and 1934 the mythical figure of the wandering Jew was rehabilitated and incorporated into the image of the eternal homeless wanderer, a figure consecrated by medieval and modern literature. The ambiguity of the term "wandering" facilitated the adaptation of the history of the Jew Ahasuerus, to the reality

146 Manoel Apolinário Pereira, *A vida do Judeu Errante*, Cordel edited by Folheria Luzeiro do Norte del gran poeta João José da Silva, s.f., 32 pages. Ruth Terra Collection, IEB/USP, cited by Jerusa Pires Ferreira, *op. cit.*; Maria Luiza Tucci Carneiro, *O Veneno da Serpente*, *op. cit.*, p. 40.

147 Manoel Apolinário Pereira, *op. cit.*, p. 31.

lived by the Jews who fled Nazi-fascism, a theme that I analyze in my book *Cidadão do Mundo: o Brasil diante do Holocausto e dos Refugiados do Nazifascismo,* 1933–1948 [Citizen of the World; Brazil in face of the Refugees of Nazifascism, 1933–1948].

MYTH 7

The Jews Are Racists

The myth says that Jews are racist. To be a racist, however, is not a privilege of one religion or another because, regardless of religious denominations, any human being can become racist. Prejudice is not an inborn feature: racism is a social phenomenon and not a genetic one. Its roots are of political, social and/or economic nature.

To understand this accusation, one must first understand what racism and especially antisemitism are. As an ideology, racism is driven by individuals or groups; it serves as an excuse for political domination and economic exploitation. Going back in time we see that, since Antiquity, men have used the existence of physical differences, political disagreements and economic interests to justify their struggles for power.

Accusing Jews of being racist is, above all, a form of covert antisemitism that contributes to erase the memory of genocide and intolerance that have been practiced against this people for centuries. However, those who use the accusation try to conceal distinctions between Jews/Israelis from Israelis/citizens. In other words, they have no interest in making such distinctions because it is upon generalizations that the myth is strengthened. Labeling the Jews as racists, Nazis or using the word "Holocaust" to refer to the conflict between Israel and Palestine, is an attempt to trivialize the genocide committed by Nazi

Germany and to minimize its consequences on the Jewish people. Given that the Holocaust was one of the sources of legitimacy for the creation of the State of Israel, to discredit it as a singular genocide in the history of humanity serves the interests of anti-Zionists. For political reasons, those who are against the existence of the State of Israel and in favor of the creation of a single State called Palestine attempt to reverse the values, and ignore the historical roots of antisemitism.

The accusation that Jews are racists earned widespread support and different versions after November 10th, 1975, when the UN General Assembly promulgated the Resolution 3379, which determined that "Zionism is a form of racism and racial discrimination". The resolution obtained 72 votes in favor,[148] 35 against[149] and 32 abstentions,[150] reflecting the ideo-

148 YES: Afghanistan, Albania, Albania, Algeria, Bahrain, Bangladesh, Brazil, Bulgaria, Burundi, Cambodia, Cameroon, Cape Verde, , Chade, Cuba, Cyprus, Czechoslovakia, Daome, Democratic Republic of Congo, Democratic Republic of Germany, Egypt, Equatorial Guinea, Gambia, Grenada, Guine Bissau, Guinea, Guyana, Hungary, India, Indonesia, Iran, Iraq, Jordan, Kuwait, Laos, Lebanon, Libya, Madagascar, Malaysia, Maldives, Mali, Malta, Mauritania, Mexico, Mongolia, Morocco, Mozambiqie, Niger, Nigeria, Northern Yemen Oman, Qatar, Somalia, Sudan, Syria, Tunisia, , Pakistan, People's Republic of China, Poland, Portugal, Rwanda, Sao Tome and Principe, Saudi Arabia, Senegal, Southern Yemen,Sri Lanka, Tanzania, Turkey, Uganda and Union of Soviet Socialist Republics, United Arab Emirates.

149 NO: Australia, Austria, Bahamas, Barbados, Belgium, Canada, Central African Republic, Costa Rica, Denmark, Dominican Republic, El Salvador, Fiji, Finland, France, Germany, Haiti, Honduras, Iceland, Israel, Italy, Ivory Coast, Liberia, Luxembourg, Malawi, Netherlands, New Zealand, Nicaragua, Norway, Panama, Republic of Ireland, Swaziland, Sweden, United Kingdom, United States of America and Uruguay

logical positions of nations opposed to the State of Israel since its creation in 1947. Some antecedents should be interpreted as precepts of an anti-Zionist movement fueled by Soviet propaganda against Israel, after the Six-Day War in 1967, and the embargo led by the Arab oil-producing states after the Yom Kippur War in 1973.

In September 2001, during the UN World Conference against Racism, Racial Discrimination, Xenophobia and Related Intolerance, held in Durban, South Africa, the UN Secretary General Kofi Annan affirmed "the belief that Zionism is racism, is dead". At that time, several countries were trying to condemn Israel for racism. The pressure came from Arab and African countries against the position taken by some Western nations:

> Resolution 77 of the Assembly of Heads of State and Government of the Organization of African Unity considered that the racist regime in [Israeli] occupied Palestine and the racist regime in Zimbabwe and South Africa have a common imperialist origin, forming a whole, with the same racist and organically connected structure in their policy aimed at suppressing the dignity and integrity of the human being.[151]

In 2009, the United Nations convened the Second World Conference against Racism [or Durban II], held in Geneva,

150 ABSTENTIONS: Argentina, Bhutan, Bolivia, Botswana, Burma, Chile, Colombia, Ecuador, Ethiopia, Gabon, Ghana, Greece, Guatemala, Jamaica, Japan, Lesotho, Mauritius, Nepal, Papua New Guinea, Paraguay, Peru, Philippines, Sierra Leone, Singapore, Thailand, Togo, Trinidad and Tobago, Venezuela, Zaire and Zambia.

151 "Sionismo não é igual a racismo". Durban, France Presse, published in *Folha de S. Paulo*, Sept. 1, 2001.

20–24 April, to review the implementation of the Durban Declaration and Programme of Action from 2001. The conference was boycotted by Australia, Canada, Germany, the Netherlands, Israel, Italy, New Zealand, Poland and the United States. The Czech Republic suspended its presence on the first day and 23 other EU countries sent unqualified delegations. The concerns from Western countries focused on the fact that the meeting would be used to promote antisemitism and anti-blasphemy laws, to encourage racism and to attack the principles of freedom of speech.

The accusation against Israel as a racist State was reopened by former Iranian President Mahmoud Ahmadinejad – the only head of state who was present at the meeting – whose statements about the Holocaust had already been controversial. For Ahamdinejad, the West used the Holocaust as a pretext for aggression against the Palestinians and referred to it as an "ambiguous and dubious question". All the delegates from the European Union countries left the conference room, while others applauded the Iranian president whose speech, as well as the boycott, were criticized by UN Secretary-General Ban Ki-moon.

The content of the speech delivered by Ahmadinejad, and the fact that it was applauded by some of the present, serves as a record of how the myth that Jews are racist [*sic*] persists and is refurbished. Ahmadinejad's opening lines synthesize, in a nutshell, his ideological stance extolling antisemitism and denialism, inciting hatred and violence against Israel and the Jews. I reproduce, here some excerpts from the beginning of Ahmadinejad's speech, and highlight some of the expressions that demonstrate the roots of several of the myths analyzed in this book.

Dear Friends, today, the human community is facing a kind of racism which has tarnished the image of humanity in the beginning of the third millennium.

World Zionism personifies racism that falsely resorts to religions and abuses religious sentiments to hide its hatred and ugly face. However, it is of great importance to bring into focus the political goals of some of the world powers and those who control huge economic resources and interests in the world. They mobilize all the resources including their economic and political influence and world media to render support in vain to the Zionist regime and to maliciously diminish the indignity and disgrace of this regime.

This is not simply a question of ignorance and one cannot conclude these ugly phenomena through consular campaigns. Efforts must be made to put an end to the abuse by Zionists and their political and international supporters and in respect with the will and aspirations of nations. Governments must be encouraged and supported in their fights aimed at eradicating this barbaric racism and to move towards reform in current international mechanisms.

There is no doubt that you are all aware of the conspiracies of some powers and Zionist circles against the goals and objectives of this conference. Unfortunately, there have been literatures and statements in support of Zionists and their crimes. And it is the responsibility of honorable representatives of nations to disclose these campaigns which run counter to humanitarian values and principles.

Speech delivered by Mahmoud Ahmadinejad during the Second World Conference Against Racism [Durban II], Geneva, April 20–24, 2009.

Today, after three UN world conferences, amidst the struggles against racism, *racial discrimination, xenophobia and related intolerance* (2001, 2009 and 2011),[152] the myth that Jews are racists survives, fueled by Israeli policy against the terrorism practiced by Hamas in Palestine. In 2001, Kofi Annan was truly optimistic when he affirmed that "the belief that Zionism is racism is dead". However, it has clearly survived, and it is possible to identify it in publications and electronic media. It suffices, for example, to look up the *Radio Islam* website, which has a "Jewish Racism" link available in 23 languages. Citations from academics and false human rights associations are some of the strategies used by those who promote this medium and thereby co-opt thousands of followers for hatred. One of the statements published there is signed by Prof. Israel Shanak, presented as "Jewish and the founder of the Israeli League of Human Rights", who would have affirmed:

> Israel as a Jewish state is a danger not only to itself and its inhabitants, but to all Jews, and to all peoples and states in the Middle East and beyond.

Sentences that are disconnected from discourse are published by Radio Islam. They emphasize that the Jews are racist, that antisemitism is an unacceptable disease and/or an extortion. Referring to the Holocaust, they assert that the "alleged persecution" is associated with a clinical pathology. Aimed at demonstrating that Jews and Israelis do not want to

152 Durbán II took place in New York, on September 22, 2011, and was boycotted by the ten aforementioned countries (including the Czech Republic), as well as Austria, Bulgaria, France and the United Kingdom.

mingle with other "races", the "radio" (mis)informs by making use, for example, of a phrase used by Rabbi Israel Meir Lau during the Annual Congress organized by the Rabbinical Centre of Europe (RCE) in the French capital, in March 2009. Presented as the former head of the rabbinate in Israel and, at the occasion, as the chairman of the Holocaust Memorial Yad Vashem, Meir Lau spoke to about three hundred rabbis saying that "*assimilation* is a threat to the future of Jews from anti-semitism and terrorism" [word underlined in the original and leading to the link: "Antisemitism is a disease"].[153] Rabbi Lau's affirmation was based on a US statistical study: "among 100 Jews of the first generation, only three are still Jews in the fourth generation". However, the Radio Islam headline for such a statement (which is real) is made in the sense of showing that "racial mixing" is seen as a threat to the Jewish people who do not want to assimilate [information distortion]. It is not disputed that the process of "assimilation" of an ethnic group implies that its identity is lost, that its traditions are erased and so on.[154]

Similarly, a set of articles on the Talmud aimed at proving that there is, in fact, Jewish racism against non-Jews. Among

---

153 Marcelo Franchi, "O anti-semitismo é uma doença? A chantagem inaceitável", in Radio Islam, http://www.radioislam.org/islam/portugues/antisem/doenca.htm. Detailed further in note 154, below.

154 The word assimilation used by Meir Lau, relates to a text by Marcelo Franchi released by Radio Islam with the title "O anti-semitismo é uma doença? A chantagem inaceitável", available on Radio Islam, http://www.radioislam.org/islam/portugues/antisem/doenca.htm. See also: "Os judeus e a 'questão racial'", on *Radio Islam*. Source: "Race-Mixing, a bigger threat to the people than terrorism", *National Journal*, published on 13.4.2009.

34. Fips, nicknamed Philipp Rupprecht, author of the images that illustrate the German antisemitic children's book *Der Giftpilz* [The Poisonous Mushroom], by Ernst Hiemer, whose text accuses Jews of racists. Caption: "It is written in the Talmud: 'Only the Jew is human. Non-Jews are not called humans, they are seen as animals', and because we Jews consider non-Jews to be animals, we refer to them only as Goy.'" Nuremberg [Bavaria], Germany, 1935. United States Holocaust Memorial Museum, ID: Collections: 1988.25.1. Available at: https://collections.ushmm.org/search/catalog/pa1069706. Access: 10.08.2019.

those texts, I quote here one of them, whose author is Reverend I. B. Pranaitis,[155] "The Talmud Unmasked". It seeks to demonstrate secret teachings regarding Christians and non-Jews. The Reverend Pranaitis quotes a phrase withdrawn from the classic work *L' Antisémitisme: son Histoire et ses Causes,* by Bernard Lazare: "The Talmud formed the Jewish Nation after the Diaspora, molded its soul, created the race".[156] Pranaitis then states that:

> *It is necessary to read and study the Talmud in order to understand International Zionism, the pride with which Jews consider themselves the masters of the world, and the power they possess to control the world's finances and media.* Revering only the golden calf, they preserve throughout several millennia their unity and their racial, political, religious and national identity, which makes them believe that they are superior beings, chosen from God, thus rejecting any kind of assimilation, and *personifying, with their way of being, the most odious form of racism.* They no longer believe in the Messiah, but only in the messianic destiny of the People of Israel, who, according to their view, their prophets and their irreducible national will, which reaches the stripes of collective paranoia, will dominate and reign over the rest of humanity. It is therefore not without reason that throughout the Bible –Old Testament– Jews are condemned for their idolatry (Ex. 32:8 – I Kings 12:28 – II Kings 17:16 – Yes. 13 – Isa. 31:6:7 – Jr. 2). Let us not

155 I. B. Pranaitis is presented as a Catholic priest, a Theology Doctor and a Professor of Hebrew at the Ecclesiastic Imperial Academia of the Roman Catholic Chruch in St. Petersburg.

156 Bernard Lazare, *L'Antisémitisme: son Histoire et ses Causes,* Edition Définitive, Paris, Editions Jean Près, 1934.

forget, therefore, Aron's warning to Moses: "Do not be angry, my Lord. You yourself know how much this people bow down to evil" (Ex. 32:22).[157]

157 I.B. Pranaitis [Reverend]. *The Talmud Unmasked*. Kindle Version.

MYTH 8

The Jews are Parasites

The myth says that the Jews are parasites, living off the work of others. By generalizing this accusation, antisemites and those who are misinformed, work together to reinforce the disfigured image that Jews do not work and do not want to work. The antisemitic saying goes, "They live like parasites on the sweat of those who work to survive and pay their taxes".

Either by convenience or ignorance, the origins of this narrative, repeated over the centuries and now part of a common language, are unknown to most people – an attribute of something that seems intuitively true. As we have previously analyzed, there are signs of an appearance or probability of truth in the ambiguous relationship between image and idea. The fact that there are Jewish tax collectors, usurers, merchants or bankers does not give others the right to accuse them of being "bloodsuckers", "parasites" or "exploiters".

From Antiquity, and for many centuries after, as a consequence of the persecutions and violence suffered along the centuries the Jews tried to seek protection from sovereigns who "charged" them for those favors in exchange of guaranteeing them security and a life. For example, emperors and their administrators regulated the value of taxes that, according to Catholic tradition, only Jews – by receiving a percentage of the value collected – could collect because their religion allowed them to make "easy profit" and "exploit others". Expenses of royal families, wars and nobility privileges were financed with taxes paid by the people. It was under this mechanism that, for centuries, during Antiquity, in Medieval and Modern times, societies functioned under the guarantees of an order imposed by those who were part of status groups.

Under laws and principles imposed by Catholicism, Jews could not own land, and were forbidden to practice agricultural activities, which were allowed to Christians who, in turn, could not engage in trade or usury. Also by imposition, Jews were allowed to collect taxes, to engage in trade and take up liberal professions that generated wealth and a privileged economic status. Since Judaism did not regard usury as a sin, many Jews enriched themsleves from tax collection and money lending by charging interest. The practice of usury led to the accusation that they "lived by exploiting their neighbors", and "made profit at the expense of the work of others". Antisemites used that social situation to stigmatize this practice, assuming it was malignant to a Catholic society. There are several texts by theologians, clergymen, philosophers, lay people and humanists who sought to demonstrate the degree of evil of Jews; those writings constitute important sources for antisemitic studies. In 1477, for example, Peter Schwartz did not spare negative adjectives to justify the persistent persecutions against Jews over the centuries:

> Jews are harshly punished from time to time. But they do not suffer innocently; they suffer because of their wickedness: for they deceive people and ruin the fields with their usury and their secret murders, as everyone knows, and that is the reason why they are persecuted, not innocently.

> There is no people more perverse, more cunning, more miserly, more reckless, more malicious, more poisonous, more angry, more deceiving and more ignominious.[158]

According to Leon Poliakov, in 16th century Germany the word *Jude* (Jewish) was already used as a synonym for usurer, the word *Judenpiess* being a homonym for *Wucher* (usury). Martin Luther himself, in his treatise *Von den Juden und ihren Lügen* [On the Jews and their Lies], written in 1543, reactivated antisemitism, and advocated for the persecution of Jews, the destruction of their religious property, as well as the confiscation of their money. Those pronouncements surfaced, especially in face of the refusal, by Jews, to convert to Protestantism.

Throughout the Modern Age – in addition to being classified as an "infectious race" by the "blood that ran through their veins" (expression used in the inquisitorial trials) – Jews were also recriminated against for their liberal and cosmopolitan positions, tendencies that associated them with the international politics of the 18th and 19th centuries. Here we find the first seedlings that, in the 19th century, would feed the false theories of a world Jewish conspiracy, and paved the way for fraudulent publications such as *The Protocols of the Elders of Zion.*

We ask: is it true that the Jews lived from tax collection? We answer: yes. But we cannot generalize: some Jews did it. Others were doctors, writers, traders, craftsmen, tailors, etc. Moreover, due to the fat that they were literate, they had more opportunities to exercise liberal activities, to become educated men, and advisors of royals who needed their knowledge.

---

158 Cited by J. Janssen, *Die Allgemeinen Zustände des Deutschen Volkes beim Augsgang des Mittelalters*, Freiburg, 1887, t. 1, p. 9. Fragment quoted by Léon Poliakov, *Du Christ aux Juifs de Cour (Histoire de l'Antisémitisme)*, Paris, Calmann-Lévy, 1955.

One more question: is it true that Jews, to "better exploit the Other", preferred to live in big cities? The answer: most of them, since the late Middle Ages, used to live in cities, but there was a reason. It was not an issue of whether they liked it or not, it was because they did not have the right to own land and, as a result, they rarely had the opportunity to live in rural areas. And when they lived in the cities, they were not so free either.

Let us refresh our memories: during the Middle Ages, according to the feudal system and consistent with the rules imposed by the Catholic Church, Jews were forced to live in ghettos or burghs. By choice? No, by imposition. In 1905, during the Council of Clermont, Pope Urban II called the First Crusade for the "liberation of the Holy Land", an expression that would culminate in a policy that unified Kingdoms in their struggle against the enemies of Christianity (read Moors and Jews). One of the slogans that impelled the Crusades was "Whoever kills a Jew will obtain the forgiveness of his sins".[159]

From the end of the 11th century onwards, Jews were isolated in Jewish quarters, as happened, for example, in Germany. After the Ecumenical Lateran Councils III and IV (1179 and 1215), restrictions imposed on Jewish communities was codified and brought together all the previous laws against the Jews. According to canons 67–70 of the Fourth Council, besides isolating Jews, prostitutes, Saracens, heretics and lepers in enclosed spaces, they were forced to wear special markings on their clothes to identify them as "infamous". But it was in France that the idea of marking the undesirables with yellow, the color-symbol of the envious and evil, was born. This strategy served to distinguish Christians from outcasts, anticipating in a

159 Wanda Kampmann, *Deutsche und Juden – Die Geschichte der Juden in Deutschland von Mittelalter bis zum Beginn des Ersten Weltkrieges*, Frankfurt, M. Fischer, 1979, p. 6.

few centuries the yellow star imposed on the latter by Nazis. England chose to introduce a symbol shaped as the saffron-colored tablets of Moses; in Italy, the Jews were forced to wear a little red hat which was later replaced by a yellow hat because the earlier enforcement was mistaken for the cardinals' hats. The circle of exclusion was further closed: Jews were forbidden to buy land and those who owned land had it confiscated. At night, Jews were to gather themselves in ghettos where gates would be set up and closed at night.

Meanwhile, in the Iberian Peninsula, Jewish community life was characterized by a certain peaceful coexistence among the peoples who lived there. However, they also ended up being excluded due to revenge, envy, or confrontation with those who wanted to enjoy the same privileges. Privileges? What were those "privileges" like and why did they have them? According to those who spread the myth, Jews were (and still are) "parasites". But to better understand the reasons behind the accusations, it is important to revisit some information, almost always ignored.

Since the 12th century, Jews made up a large proportion of the population that inhabited the Iberian Peninsula and were devoted to agriculture and commerce. Organized in communities – the largest of those being Santarém – they had a separate cultural life and constituted a different class because of their customs and religion. Christians who insisted on honoring their traditions, also lived that way. The Jewish communes (note: Jewish) were subject to heavy tax burdens which constituted an important source of income for the Royal Treasury. To be allowed to live in the country, Jews were forced to pay a *per capita* contribution known as *juderega* or *judenga*. They also paid to the Crown the Rabbinate tax, and to their neighbors, tolls, taxes on the use of pastures and custom taxes. The latter three, for example, were common during the Middle Ages and not exclusive to Jews. It was a practice that regulated fiefdoms and guaranteed dividends to feudal lords who, in return, offered protection to their subjects. For those who have studied some Middle Ages history, it will not be difficult to recall the concept of fiefdom. But the treatment of Jews was different. Let us see the reasons for the cases of those who lived in the Iberian Peninsula.

In 1353, King D. Alfonso IV enacted a law obliging Jews to pay a high annual amount called *Serviço Real dos Judeus* [Royal Service of Jews] to which were added three hundred thousand pounds annually. The inhabitants of those communities were wealthy and "aristocratic" Jews, as well as small merchants, artisans, lawyers, real estate brokers, tax collectors and financiers. The vast majority lived in urban centers, exploring small commerce and usury. Those who lived in rural areas dedicated themselves to the professions of muleteers and shopkeepers, a kind of travelers who, carrying boxes of fabric in their mules, went door to door offering their articles.[160]

Up to that time, contrary to the restrictions enforced by the Ecumenical Councils in some European countries, Jews who lived in the Iberian Peninsula did not use badges to differentiate themselves from Christians. Relationships of sociability became damaged by religious differences, and Jews were favored by the ancient Foral who guaranteed them a certain mobility.[161] Protected by royal determinations, Jews often enjoyed a favorable legal status, with certain privileges. But nothing came free of

160 Maria Luiza Tucci Carneiro, *Preconceito racial em Portugal, op. cit.*, pp. 29–34.

161 Foral was a royal document used in Portugal, aimed at establishing a municipality and regulating its administration, duties and privileges.

charge: thanks to their knowledge and experience, they were recognized as skillful financiers and, as such, were hired to official positions during the reign of Sancho II (1223–1248), which contradicted the rules of exclusion imposed by Pope Gregory IX.

Thus, the restrictions instigated by the clergy were applied by D. Afonso IV (1325–1357) who reaffirmed, in 1325, a law that required Jews to wear badges and prohibited the use of gold and silver necklaces. In 1325, the King took away their right to emigrate and, the following year, he organized the tax office of the Jewish communes. Between 1357 and 1367, D. Pedro I imposed severe penalties on usury, which did not prevent some Jews from maintaining large fortunes. But note the following detail: some Jews, but also some Catholics. The majority of the population lived in a miserable way, without privileges and frightened by Catholic preaching that threatened them with a future life (after death) in Hell. To heretics, the bonfire![162]

Dark times announced that the situation of Jews in the Iberian Peninsula was changing for the worse, effacing the image of coexistence between the three religions: Catholics, Jews and Muslims. Disorders broke out in Portugal when, during the reign of Ferdinand (1397–1383), Jews were subjected to ill-treatment and laws were violated. After the King's death, his widow, D. Leonor, took over as regent, but, pressured by the elites in Lisbon, she restricted the privileges of Jews and dismissed a large number of them from public office. With the ascension to the throne of D. João, *Mestre de Avis,* in 1385, the followers of Judaism returned to a period of peace and tranquility, despite the contrary actions carried out by the religious cast.

---

162 Meyer Kaiserling, *História dos Judeus em Portugal,* São Paulo, Pioneira, 1971, pp. 5, 7–10 and 22.

In Spain, the situation was even more serious: in 1391, attacks too place against the Jewish quarters and massacres of Jews resulted. Terror spread throughout Castile, Aragon, Catalonia, Valencia and Seville. Those who were not killed because of their religious resistance were forced to accept baptism; some adopted false names and took refuge in Portugal, where they received protection by King D. João. There, some continued to serve as doctors and surgeons in the palace or were hired as tax collectors, for their knowledge and experience, which distinguished them from Catholics.[163] But they were forced to live in isolated Jewish quarters, albeit within the walls of the city.

Since antisemitism was a long-standing phenomenon, whose manifestations and motifs varied from time to time and place, the Jews remained united in their common beliefs and traditions. This union, in many situations, went beyond the principles of Judaism and projected itself as a way of defending Jewish communities in exile. Distant from their homeland (the ancient Palestine), Jews sought to "maintain their integrity as a people despite all the adversities of the diaspora, marked by massacres, rape and looting.[164] Because of their strong communitarian identity, they were considered a "self-enclosed people", accused of forming true "racial cysts" and "bodies foreign to the nation".

Between the 15th and 20th centuries – following the trajectory of the narratives – those type of expressions became typical of antisemite, nationalist xenophobes or anti-Zionists, who interpret this "enclosure" as a form of racism [*sic*]. It is turning

163 Albert Sicroff, *Les Controvers des Status de Pureté de Sang en Espagne du XVe au XVIIe Siècle*, Paris, Libraire Marcel Didier, 1960, p. 9.

164 Rabbi Y. David Weitman, "Introdução: O Significado Profundo da Dispersão e das Migrações do Povo Judeu", in *Recordações da Imigração Judaica em S. Paulo*, São Paulo, Maayanot, 2013, pp. 9–18.

the story upside down, and effacing the process of exclusion that forced Jews to live in isolation, marked as outcasts for centuries. But, for those who discriminate it is opportune to forget, deny and/or "assassinate the memory", as stated by Vidal-Naquet in his work, which helps us to understand the persistence and dynamics of myths.[165]

From 1933 onwards, the concept of permissiveness of the Jewish people gained ground in the discourse of the National Socialists in Germany who, through sophisticated strategies articulated by the Ministry of Enlightenment and Propaganda led by Joseph Goebbels, reinforced the image of Jews as "parasites". This accusation was coupled with the idea that they formed true cancers in the nations where they settled, was directly associated with the opinion that Jews, in a figurative sense, corrupted, corroded and consumed the Nation slowly and secretly. Using a vocabulary extracted from the medical discourse, Jews were identified as "sick beings", a centuries-old metaphorical composition. It is worth remembering in the context of the myths discussed here that at different times during the Middle Ages and in modern times, Jews had their image compared to the proliferation of diseases, including the plague and leprosy.

Heresy, epidemics and Judaism were often used in the traditional antisemitic discourse with a sense of malignancy, permissiveness, and other stigma.[166] Thus, these "diseases"

165 Pierre Vidal-Naquet, *Les assassins de la mémoire: "Un Eichmann de papier" et autres éssais sur le révisionisme*, Paris, Seuil, 1995.

166 Yara Nogueira Monteiro, *Da Maldição Divina à Exclusão Social: Um Estudo da Hanseníase em São Paulo*, Doctoral Thesis in Social History, History Departament, FFLCH, University of São Paulo, 1995; Yara Nogueira Monteiro; Maria Luiza Tucci Carneiro, *As Doenças e os Medos Sociais*, São Paulo, Editora Unifesp, 2013.

35. Fips, pseudonym Philipp Rupprecht, author of the image depicting a German shop being cheated by a Jewish merchant. Caption: "You have people who do this to you, too. But it wasn't meant to be that way!" Germany, 1936–1937. United States Holocaust Memorial Museum, courtesy of Alex Kertesz. Available at: https://collections.ushmm.org/search/catalog/irn8224. Access: 10.09.2019.

36. Unidentified author. Symbolic image of the plague that illustrates Herman Esser's book, *Die Jüdische Weltpest* [The Jewish World Plague]. Munich, Zentralverlag der NSDAP, 1939 [Cover]. Tucci Collection/ State of São Paulo/Brazil.

were assimilated by the National Socialists, who sought to justify the prophylaxis demanded by the Aryan community: extermination of the social canker (in that case, the Jews), calls to radical and eliminationist solutions (Final Solution) – cures for a "disease" that had been diagnosed as irreversible. This is the tone of the book *Die Jüdische Weltpest* (The Jewish World Plague), published in 1939 by Herman Esser

(1900–1981), a publisher, propagandist and one of Hitler's main allies.[167]

That same version of the myth found followers in Brazil where the "virus" was associated with the "uninterrupted arrival of waves of Jewish refugees from Nazism" and whose "infiltration" into the social body needed to be combated. What does that mean? To shut the harbors to them as well as to the possibility to obtain visas. The Jews were seen by diplomats, especially those on missions abroad, as "bodies who were foreign to the nation" and could cause political, economic and social unrest. As a summary of the idea that Jewish refugees lived at the expense of the exploitation of the Other, the Brazilian ambassador in Berlin wrote to Oswaldo Aranha, the Foreign Minister of Vargas' government:

> They are negative elements in their homeland community and from which they only seek profit. They are not useful and have never been useful to Brazil, nor do they contribute to the country's public or private economy. They are exploiters of nationality and do not have and cannot have any sincere sentiment with regard to it.[168]

167 Herman Esser, *Die Jüdische Welpest,* Munich, Zentralverlag der NSDAP, 1939.

168 Memo by Muniz de Aragão, Brazilian ambassador in Berlin, to Foreign Minister Oswaldo Aranha, Berlin, April 26, 1938. Ref. 511.14 (193). AHI/RJ.

MYTH 9

The Jews Control the Media

The myth says that the Jews control the media. This statement – according to the antisemites – is part of a supposed "program for the conquest of the world by the Jews", a thread that runs from the Protocols of the Elders of Zion, whose content attends the most varied political interests.

From the moment the *Protocols of the Elders of Zion* were launched in Tsarist Russia, they disseminated the idea of a secret plot articulated by the international Jewish community whose aim was, allegedly, to destroy Christianity and to establish the Mosaic-Talmudic faith as a universal religion. This would guarantee their path to seize the power in the Western World. One of the first explanations made public through the *Moskvu* magazine (n. 1) on September 23rd, 1919, was that the Bolshevik Revolution, according to historian Norman Cohn, "had received a subsidy of many millions of dollars from the American banker Jacob Schiff on behalf of the New York group of Kuhn, Loeb & Co., and that this had enabled them to carry out their revolution."[169] That information had been taken from a document written by Schiff in 1905 in which "he tried to persuade the United States Government to exert itself on behalf of the Russian Jews".[170]

169 Norman Cohn, *op. cit.*, p. 138.

170 *Ibidem.*

Beginning in 1919, the various editions of the *Protocols* began to include accusations that the secret plot, besides being Jewish, was also communist. Printed copies in different languages were disseminated in England, Italy, France and the United States, in order to convince the governments of those nations of the importance of intensifying their interventions in Russia. The intention behind the narrative was to show that Russia had not been shaken by a civil war but by an international Jewish conspiracy. In a short time, despite being denounced as a forgery by journalist Phillip Graves in a series of articles published in the *London Times* in 1922,[171] the *Protocols* was published in Germany by Ludwig Müller (whose pseudonym was Gottfried zur Beck), a retired army captain and the editor of the conservative and antisemitic magazine *Auf Vorposten*. In France, the *Protocols* were disseminated thanks to Monsignor Jouin, who was determined to spread the idea of a "crusade" against the Jewish-Masonic danger. From the publication of this editorial onwards, the homonymous book reinforced the antisemitic discourse that became stronger and stronger in Western Europe. In Berlin, two Russians – Pyotr Nikolaevich Shabelsky-Bork and Fyodor Viktorivich Vinberg – would be responsible for publishing the full 1911 edition of Sergei Nilus's text, which contributed to transform fanaticism into an obsession: the need to get rid of the Jews to prevent the proliferation of the Jewish-Masonic-Bolshevik conspiracy. The first edition of the Protocols in Germany was published in January 1920 with the title *Die Geheimnisse der Weisen von Zion* [The Secrets of the Wise Men of Zion], by the Verband gegen die Überhebung des

171 As Norman Cohn observes, the propagandists of the *Protocols* assured the publication's authenticity, based on the indication that "at the British Museum Library there was an original copy of Nilus' book [*sic*]. Norman Cohn, *op. cit.*, p. 151.

Judentums [Association against the Presumption of the Jews], directed by the same Gottfried zur Beck.[172]

The prevailing idea around the *Protocols* was that a world-wide network of Jewish-Masonic organizations was being articulated by a group of old Jewish sages from Zion since the 18th century. According to the narrative, few intellectuals escaped being coopted by the Jews: Rousseau, Voltaire, Tolstoy, Gorki, the encyclopedists, etc.; all of them were paid to plot a revolution on behalf of the Jews. The accusations, which were adapted and updated in each new edition of the *Protocols,* were unlimited. According to the narrative, for example, the *Alliance Israelite Universelle* [Universal Israelite Alliance] was the secret counsel of the *Wise Men of Israel.* Another allegation was that World War I had been financed by Jews. More recently, in the 1991 edition, the *Protocols* blame the Jews for corruption, drugs, prostitution, AIDS etc.[173] The list goes on.

According to the original text, the *Protocols* – translated into Portuguese with commentaries by Gustavo Barroso, in 1936 – the world press had been "bought" by the Jews, who are defined as a "brute and blind force", a "masquerade force" that manipulates the "unguided" people, who are "weakened by liberalism". In short: they [the Jews] are "men oriented by their petty passions, their superstitions...", a kind of anarchy that ruins governments...", "excited by their thirst for power...", "worms that gnaw at the prosperity of non-Jews...."[174]

172 Norman Cohn, *op. cit.*, p. 147.

173 *Protocolos dos Sábios de Sião,* Coleção Comemorativa do Centenário de Gustavo Barroso (5th reedition), Porto Alegre, Editora Revisão, 1991. See the full listo of the Brazilian editions of this book in, Maria Luiza Tucci Carneiro, *O Veneno da Serpente, op. cit.*, pp. 59–68.

174 *Ibidem*, pp. 86–87.

Aware of the role of the press, the *Protocols* would propose the creation of a society "at the disposal of our international agents, who have thousands of eyes and no borders can stop them". According to the Elders of Zion:

> In the hands of the States of to-day there is a great force that creates the movement of thought in the people, and that is the Press. The part played by the Press is to keep pointing out requirements supposed to be indispensable, to give voice to the complaints of the people, to express and create discontent. It is in the Press that the triumph of freedom of speech finds its incarnation. But the goyim States have not known to make use of this force; and it has fallen into our hands. Through the Press we have gained the power of influence while remaining ourselves in the shade: thanks to the Press we have got gold in our hands, notwithstanding that we have had to gather it out of the oceans of blood and tears. But it has paid us, though we have sacrificed many of our people.
>
> We turn to the periodical press. We shall impose on it, as on all printed matter, stamp taxes per sheet and deposits of caution-money, and books of less than 30 sheets will pay double. We shall reckon them as pamphlets in order, on the one hand, to reduce the number of magazines, which are the worst form of printed poison, and, on the other, in order that this measure may force writers into such lengthy productions that they will be little read especially as they will be costly.
>
> Literature and journalism are the two most important educational powers; for this reason, our government will buy up the greater number of periodicals. By these means we shall neutralize the bad influence of the private and

obtain an enormous influence over the human mind. If we were to allow ten private periodicals we should ourselves start thirty, and so forth.

The need for daily bread forces the goyim to keep silence and be our humble servants. Agents taken on to our press from among the goyim will at our orders discuss anything which it is inconvenient for us to issue directly in official documents, and we meanwhile, quietly amid the din of the discussion so raised, shall simply take and carry through such measures as we wish and then offer them to the public as an accomplished fact.[175]

By insisting on press control as a means to dominate the spirits (read consciousness), the text of the *Protocols* left a negative legacy: they contributed (and still contribute) to incite hatred and make believe that Jews control the media. Old editions are still available online or are sold in second-hand bookstores. In several countries which are enemies of Israel, new editions of the *Protocols* continue to be published and act as one of the poisons of contemporary antisemitism. The pernicious influence of this myth, which creates traps and interferes with the minds of the less informed, can hardly be measured.

Over the Internet, it is possible to access texts published by *Radio Islam,* which insists that the international media are controlled by Jews. A long list of names and companies is constantly updated, disseminating lies and denialism. *Radio Islam,* for example, is anxious to point out that "some instruments of the international media are really important in forming

175 *Ibidem,* pp. 100, 158, 159, 165. English version of the extracts: https://web.archive.org/web/20140729103854/http://ddickerson.igc.org/The_Protocols_of_the_Learned_Elders_of_Zion.pdf. Retrieved: August 20, 2018.

37. "The US press is 97% in the hands of the Jews", headline of the *Great Anti-Masonic Exposition*. Belgrade (Serbia), 1941. United States Holocaust Memorial Museum, courtesy of the Katz Family. Available at: https://collections.ushmm.org/search/catalog/irn542645. Access: 10.08.2019.

the minds of the people and earn a lot in Brazil through cable TV sets ... [...] Among the best known names are Walt Disney Company, Red ESPN (as part of the Disney empire), Time Warner, Inc., HBO (a subsidiary of Time Warner), Blockbuster, which distributes thousands of movies in Brazil, Showtime, MTV, [and] Nickelodeon networks [which] also belong to Viacom, Inc." They also call the attention to the fact that "American Jews gave us the cartoon Beavis and Butthead, which helps burn the minds of thousands of our youngsters".[176]

On *Facebook, Twitter, YouTube, Dailymotion, Instagram* and several other social media websites, one can find sophisticated antisemitic videos that seek to reinforce the idea that Zionists

176 Radio Islam, http://www.radioislam.org/islam/portugues/poder/jud"os_brasil.htm. Retrieved, Sept. 10, 2013.

control the media, that the *Protocols of the Sages of Zion* are "true and still current", that Jews are "murderous animals", or that "the Holocaust is a big lie".[177] Many of those statements operate as political strategies in the struggle against the existence of the State of Israel, a discourse maintained especially by radical Islam.

The update of the myth that the Jews dominate the media can be seen in a caricature published by the German daily *Süddeutsche Zeitung* in Munich on February 21st, 2014 and replicated by the *Jüdische Allgemeine* – Germany's largest Jewish newspaper – and in the Austrian press. The image shows Mark Zuckerberg represented as an octopus, whose tentacles control the social networks, marked with the *Facebook* and *WhatsApp* logos. This is the animalization of the myth that, once again, stigmatizes the image of the Jew, demonized by his power and fortune, although most benefit from his inventions. It is at this moment that the power of the myth obscures reality.

177 Video *Dailymotion*: "Sionistas dominan a mídia no Brasil": http://www.dailymotion.com/video/xyvu7u_os-protocolos-dos-sabios-de-siao-parte-7-de-7-nova-ordem-mundial-e-religioes_animals. Retrieved: June 1, 2018.

MYTH 10

The Jews Manipulate the United States

The myth says that Jews and the government of Israel manipulate and lead the U.S. government. Such an argument feeds the myth of the international Jewish plot, anti-Zionism and antisemitism. It is a cumulative narrative and a successor of accusations that ignore a set of historical facts that, since the 17th century, have brought Jews closer to the American nation.

Based on its content, this myth – like so many others – provides subsidies for an "essay on the blindness of antisemites" and on the demonization process of the United States and Israel. The images that depict the myth, generalize and omit certain historical facts that cut across the U.S.–Israel relations and disregard the actuality that, between the two countries, there are convergences and divergences, as pointed out by historian and professor of International Relations Samuel Feldberg.[178] It is important to remember that both countries have a common cultural and ideological identity in defending democratic values and as inheritors of centuries-old Jewish traditions. The

178 Samuel Feldberg, *Estados Unidos e Israel: uma aliança em questão*. São Paulo, Hucitec, 2008. See also: https://www.researchgate.net/publication/33760849_Estados_Unidos_da_America_e_Israel_uma_alianca_em_questao

strong presence of Jews in the United States cannot be underestimated as it goes back to 1654, when the first North American Jewish community, founded by 24 fugitive Jews from Recife, Brazil – most of them of Sephardic origin – landed on the island of Manhattan and established in the Dutch colony of New Amsterdam a trading post of the West Indian Company in the New World. In March 1655, five other families and three single men arrived in New Amsterdam directly from Holland, followed by hundreds more. Although the Treaty of Breda (1667) guaranteed religious freedom to Jews, and the right to individual and commercial property, they were forbidden to build synagogues and had to pay taxes to the Anglican Church. Their residences functioned as houses of prayer in order to form the *minianim* and maintain their religious traditions.

On the eve of the American War of Independence, Jews could neither work in public institutions nor vote. Only after the independence of the United States, in 1776, did American Jews have their civil and religious freedom secured by the Declaration of Independence, which reinforced the ideas of freedom and justice by stating that "all men are created equal".

The reality of that relationship, however, outweighs the fact that the United States almost always defends Israel, the Jews and Judaism. Traditionally – and I do not consider this as an issue to be assessed in the light of imperialism or colonialism – the United States has always defended universal values such as freedom of religion and has publicly criticized the recent escalation of attacks on minorities, including Islamic minorities such as Shiites and Ahmadis in Indonesia and Baha'is in Iran. The United States has always defended freedom of religion as an innate right of every human being, a position assumed in the country's annual reports on the subject. Heavy criticism has been levelled, for example, in Saudi Arabia – another ally of the American nation – where religious freedom is widely suppressed.[179]

One may consider the myth that "Jews manipulate and are led by the United States" as supported by three basic accusations: 1) the Jews hold an immense power and unparalleled influence in the United States; 2) The "Jewish lobby" is a decisive factor in the United States' support for Israel; 3) Jewish-Zionist interests are not identical to American interests and are in constant conflict.

Reviewing diplomatic, law enforcement and Catholic documents produced in the 20th century, we find examples that help to understand how this narrative is constructed. It suffices to take up some of the myths analyzed in this breviary to confirm that there is always the conscious manipulation of a set of metaphors and analogies that offer support to the lie. The fabrication of such arguments shows that we are still heirs of a totalitarian logic that, during Nazism, was based on ethnic and class differences aimed at dominating large parts of the population, as was analyzed by Hannah Arendt in her classic work *The Origins of Totalitarianism*. It is worth remembering that totalitarian propaganda was marked by conspiracy theories and a fictitious reality in order to seduce the masses and justify the extermination of the Jews.[180]

This myth is directly correlated to the argument used by National Socialists to demonstrate that the "world Jewry" conspired against Germany and is associated with the United

179 "EUA denunciam a escalada de ódio contra judeus e muçulmanos", in Portal Terra, May 20th, 2013. http://noticias.terra.com.br/mundo/estados-unidos/eua-denunciam-escalada -do-odio-contra-judeus-e-muçulmanos,4dcaaa33a92ce310VgnCLD2000000ec6eb0aRCRD.html

180 Hannah Arendt, *The Origins of Totalitarianism*, New York, Schocken Books, 1951.

States. That was the approach used by Wolfgang Diewerge, a member of the Council and the head of the Radio Division of the Ministry of Propaganda and Popular Enlightenment in Nazi Germany, who published a booklet entitled *The War Goal of World Plutocracy. A Documentary Publication on the Book by the President of the American Federation of Peace Theodore Nathan Kaufman,* "Germany Must Perish". In his text, Diewerge introduces Kaufman as one of the Jewish leaders, who was well known in the United States for being a member of Roosevelt's advisory group. The writing propagandistic goal, according to an analysis presented by Enrique Luz, was to "make the gathering of allied leaders a senseless event, and to transform it into a Jewish machination". This accusation was reinstated in the pamphlet entitled *Niemals!* [Never!], published by Heinrich Goitsch on October/November 1944, with a print run of about 400,000 copies.[181]

In a true reversal of their own genocidal purposes and actions, the pamphlet alerts the German people to that particular moment of defeat and suffering caused by Jews who, from biblical times, up to that time, had allegedly murdered several peoples:

> The German people must know that, at that time, unimaginable suffering was about to fall on us, Germans. We would have been disarmed, occupied, economically plundered, divided into small states, dominated and ruled by the Bolsheviks, Americans and English, forced to send ten million German men to the Soviet Union and other countries for forced labor, obliged to send our children, our most precious goods, to the whole world, to be sterilized

181 Enrique Luz, *op. cit.*

> by Jewish doctors, castrated, rendered sterile, so that the German people may literally come to perish in a few decades, forced to renounce the national-socialist ideal that we carry in our hearts as the ideal of the century.

The accusation that Jews manipulated allied countries during the World War II was printed on a poster published in occupied France in 1942. Behind the flags of Great Britain, the United States and the Soviet Union emerges the figure of a fat Jew, elegantly dressed, which proves to be a man of great political influence and economic standing. As is the case in most Nazi propaganda images, a Star of David – in this particular picture, it hangs from a huge clockwork chain – the symbol identifies the man as Jewish, unorthodox, adapted to the American life. The three flags form a kind of curtain used to cover the illustrious man who spies, is powerful, and just waiting to enter the scene.[182]

This narrative remains and has been rehabilitated by a new wave of antisemitism that reverberates hatred and intolerance in this 21st century. Its adherents, day after day, appropriate pan-Arabic, anti-Zionist and anti-Americanist accusations that echo in the conflicts between Israel and Palestine. It is a speech that survives, in large part, fueled by videos, photographs, cartoons and journalistic texts with widespread opinions about the crisis in the Middle East that has the United States as a traditional mediator.

Back to some historical records: in June 1937, diplomat Oswaldo Aranha (1894–1960), the Brazilian ambassador to the United States between 1934 and 1937, wrote to Getúlio Vargas speaking about the Spanish Civil War (1936–1939). Even though Aranha is still seen as an ardent champion of the rela-

---

182 *Ibidem.*

38. "In the bosom of Abraham," *Revista Careta*, Rio de Janeiro, April 30, 1938, n. 1558 [Cover]. Tucci Collection/ State of São Paulo/Brazil.

tions between Brazil and the United States as well as a personal friend of President Roosevelt, Aranha insisted on the idea that "there was a richer, more active and cunning international force that would end up dominating the Americans". That force, in his opinion, was nothing more than Judaism, which, in his opinion, controlled the United States, and would eventually lead the country to the side where the Jewish interest was. He concluded that everything was "the work of the Jewish opinion and of workers' pressure", an accusation in vogue in the speeches of right-wing groups and of several Brazilian Catholic intellectuals.[183]

The image of the United States represented by the cartoon character of "Uncle Sam" – as a protector of the Jews – was a fixture in Brazilian illustrated magazines during the 1930s and 1940s, among them the magazine *Careta*. On the front cover of the April 30th,1938 issue, for example, the figure of an apparently uncommitted "Uncle Sam" is spying a group of cornered Israelis, sheltered under an umbrella that displays the flags of Latin American countries, including Brazil. The title of the cartoon is "Abraham Breast"; it conducts the reader to the web of relations between the United States and the Jews. Outside the scene, the Brazilian "Jeca"[184] talks with "Jacob" (a Jewish refugee with a hooked nose and the "eyes of a bird of prey"), and praises the United States' camaraderie, which, at that time, encouraged the League of Nations to welcome Jews expelled and/or persecuted by Nazism. The subtitle mocks the fact with the following commentary: "Yes, yes, but the umbrella is not yours!" The theme of the United States as a nation that protected Jews is taken up again a few months later by the same newspaper that, on the cover, shows children, old people and adult immigrants

183 Letters from Oswaldo Aranha, Brazilian Ambassador in the United States to Getúlio Vargas, President of Brazil. Washington, 10.05.1937, 19.05.1937 y 4.6.37, p.2. Folders OA 37.05.19; OA 37.05.19; and OA 37.06.04/3. CPDOC/RJ.

184 Just like Macunaíma – a character from the novel by the same name penned by Mario de Andrade – the figure of *Jeca Tatu* became one of the icons of Brazility. The latter was conceived by Monteiro Lobato, a well-known Brazilian author and publisher who, in 1914, wrote for the newspaper *O Estado de S. Paulo* the article "Urupês"; there, he referred to this character as a "plague" to be fought since he was responsible for burning the Brazilian forests, was lazy and a parasite. In 1918, *Jeca Tatu* was used as a symbol of a public health campaign in the interior of Brazil, and also to illustrate the advertisements of a "miraculous fortifier": *Biotônico Fontoura*.

39. Hanisc, author of the poster entitled "Behind the Powers of the Enemy: The Jew", c. 1941–1942. Here the Jew is a conspirator plotting for world domination and acting behind the scenes of nations at war with Germany. This caricature represents the "Jewish financier" that manipulates the Allies, i.e., Great Britain, the United States, and the Soviet Union. United States Holocaust Memorial Museum, courtesy of Helmut Eschwege. ID Collections: 1990.193.9. Available at: https://collections.ushmm.org/search/catalog/irn2910. Access: 10.08.2019.

among suitcases, domestic artifacts, clothes and trunks, rubbing shoulders trying to fit inside "Uncle Sam's" hat and umbrella. Insecurity and anguish mark the aimless gaze of the Jewish characters created by cartoonist J. Carlos.[185]

In the 1990s, the myth still reverberated in the writings by revisionist writer Siegfried Ellwanger Castan (1928–2010) who, in several works, reproduces a racist and conspiratory logic adopted by extreme-right groups. Castan was an insistent defender of the myth of the Jewish conspiracy that, led by the United States, aimed at destroying the world.[186]

Even the fateful September 11, 2001 did not escape the antisemitic discourse, disguised as anti-Americanism. After the terrorist attacks on the World Trade Center (New York) and the Pentagon (Washington, DC), intellectuals, journalists and academics (including Brazilians) celebrated the act of terror via outbursts of antisemitism. By attempting to reveal the vulnera-

---

185 *Revista Careta*, Rio de Janeiro, n. 1558, Apr. 1938 [cover]; n.1591, Dec. 1938 [cover]. B.M.M.A/SP

186 In 1986, Siegfried Ellwanger Castan was reported to the *Coordinadoria das Promotorias Criminais* (Criminal Prosecutor's Office) in Porto Alegre, Brazil, for inciting hatred through his works published by the *Editora Revisão*, which he owns. Authored by him: *Holocausto Judeu or Alemão?*, *Nos Bastidores da Mentira do Século*, by Castan himself, *Hitler Culpado ou Inocente?* by Sérgio Oliveira and *Os Protocolos dos Sábios de Sião*, with a preface by Gustavo Barroso. New charges in 1990 led to the establishment of a police investigation, which was referred to the Public Prosecutor's Office and, in 1995, he was tried and acquitted. A year later, he was unanimously convicted by the High Court Judges of the Third Criminal Chamber of the State of Rio Grande do Sul Court of Justice. A new complaint was received in 1998, which culminated in him being sentenced to two years in prison for the crime of racism. Castan then appealed, arguing that Jews are an ethnicity and not a race and, therefore, anti-Semitism is not racism. His appeal, however, was denied, and the conviction was reiterated by the Federal Superior Court in 2003.

bility of U.S. imperialism, and accusing Israel of "terrorism" and "genocide", those citizens broke one of the snake's eggs. The aesthetic impact of aircraft puncturing the towers surpassed the concept of a terrorist attack. Among the rumors that circulated to explain the causes, I personally heard from a group of university students that Jews and Israelis were involved in that act, since on September 11th "several members of the Jewish community had not gone to work at the World Trade Center". According to them, that would explain the small number of Jews who died in the attack.

Those kinds of accusations serve to further demonize the United States, Israel and the Jews, with the use of images that portray the suffering of the Palestinian people, mainly by means of photographs that are often manipulated and decontextualized. Moreover, there is the distorted concept of Zionism, widely used by the media, which portrays Israel as "the spearhead of Yankee imperialism in the Middle East, a simple instrument for the oppression of the Arab people by the Americans", as defined by Moses Storch in an article published on September 20th, 2001. From his point of view, the press ignores certain historical facts and hastily uses the Arab population of Palestine that, over the course of more than half a century of suffering, has been used as cannon fodder for the interests of the most authoritarian and reactionary Arab regimes. Storch makes a counterpoint between Zionist ideology and the pan-Arabic ideology, which he characterizes as being:

> [...] developed to perpetuate the domination, by small but powerful elites and casts, of vast populations of dispossessed and oppressed people; they have manipulated their (mis)information and (mis)education systems to attribute to the "Zionist entity" (the Little Satan) and to the United

States (the "Great Satan") the origin of all evils, and diverting peoples' attention from the real origins of their misery.[187]

The Iranian government has emphatically, persistently and dangerously expressed the character of U.S.–Israeli relations, using humor and sarcasm to reinforce antisemitic myths. An example of this incitement to hatred can be found in the cartoons presented at a competition and exhibition inaugurated at the Palestinian Museum in Tehran on August 15th, 2006. Under the curatorship of Masud Shoyai Tobatai, director of the Iranian Caricature House, 204 works of authorship by caricaturists were selected from different countries: Brazil, Belgium, Bulgaria, Canada, USA, England, Italy, Spain, Holland and Norway. Among the names, are those of Italian Alessandro Gato, American Matt Gaver, Russian Raul Erkimbaiev and Brazilian Carlos Latuf.

The demonization of the United States and of the State of Israel is explicit in the caricature of Russian Raul Erkimbaiev. There we see a Jew (a symbol of the State of Israel) and a "Statue of Liberty" (a symbol of the United States). Both characters have claw hands and traits that give them an animalistic, monstrous identity. The Jew, in the foreground, walks carefully on tiptoes, throwing bombs on a city outlined by several religious temples. In one of his arms, he brings a band with the symbol of a gear that reminds of a Nazi swastika. His face is totally deformed by his hooked nose, thick lips and bulging eyes,

---

187 Moisés Storch, "A Satanização dos Estados Unidos e de Israel e a Manipulação do Sofrimento Palestino", published on September 20, 2001 on http://pazagora.org/2001/09/a-satanizacao-dos-estados-unidos-e-de-israel-e-a-manipulacao-do-sofrimento-palestino/. Retrieved: June, 1, 2018.

like a bird of prey. He has a helmet from which come out two *peyote* (plural of the Hebrew word *pe'ah* which designates the curls on the sides of the hair, characteristic of Orthodox Jews), which end up in the shape of a spearhead. To the right, several buildings in ruins and a cemetery make up the scene of tragedy and death. Dark smoke rolls are diluted to form a "Statue of Liberty" that emerges behind the Jew (Israel), signaling Israel's image as the "spearhead of Yankee imperialism in the Middle East".[188]

The "Statue of Liberty", crowned by the seven-pointed headband, has its symbols carefully deformed by the cartoon's author: the traditional torch is drawn in the form of a burning bone that helps to ignite the bombs thrown by "Israel". The book he holds in his left hand is identified as the Talmud, thus completing the three Masonic symbols idealized by Frédéric Auguste Bartholdi, sculptor of the true Statue of Liberty (opened in 1886 and offered to the United States as a gift from the French): the torch, the book and the seven-pointed tiara.

To ignore and manipulate historical facts is part of the discursive strategy of the creators of myths; myth makers do not hesitate to invent situations in such a way that their messages divert to sources of tension. Samuel Feldberg – who we have already mentioned – gives some examples in that direction, demonstrating that U.S.–Israeli relations only began to grow closer "after the Six-Day War in 1967, and within the context of the Vietnam War and the Nixon Doctrine, when the United States came to support various regions of the world, without sending troops". As examples of those divergences, he relates a set of facts: that President Truman faced strong opposition from the State Department and the Pentagon, even though the United

188 *Ibidem.*

States had supported the creation of the State of Israel; that Israel fought with French armament in the Six Day War; that in 1973, during the Yom Kippur War, the Americans supported Israel to counteract the ex-USSR's support for Arabs; and that the United States pressured Israel in order to prevent their reaction during the Gulf War, in 1991, when Iraq launched missiles into its territory.[189]

40. [The image is not reproduced here, but can be viewed via the link below]. Raul Erkimbaiev, caricaturist, author of the antisemitic cartoon presented at the contest and exhibition organized by the Iranian House of Cartoon, curated by Masud Shoyai Tobatai at the Tehran Art Museum, 2006. The second exhibit opened in June 14, 2016. https://www.irancartoon.com/site/gallery?page=1

Facts like these serve to strengthen the accusations that Jews – because of their conspiratory power and leadership capacity – manipulate the United States by maintaining a pro-Israel lobby in Washington. There is a rebirth of the traditional accusation by modern antisemites that Jews form a "State within the State", an expression that is already found in inquisitorial discourses and used to justify the persecution of Jews in the Iberian Peninsula especially between the 15th and 18th centuries. In the 21st century there is an inversion of this accusatory approach, that updates the myth: it is said that the United States are manipulated by the Jews, led by an ultra-secret organization called Kahila or "the diabolical brain", which is

189 Samuel Feldberg, "Israel y EUA", conference delivered at the cycle *Israel e o Mundo*, Centro da Cultura Judaica, São Paulo, September 10th, 2013, https://coletivojudaico.wordpress.com/category/centro-de-cultura-judaica/page/2/ . Retrieved: June 1, 2018.

> allegedly composed of three hundred devils or representatives of Satan, according to the version propagated by Fahti-el-Ibyari, an author of several anti-Semitic books.

According to Bila Sorj, one of the leading scholars of anti-Semitism in the 21st century, such a stream of stereotyped images of Jews is produced especially by the media in Saudi Arabia, Jordan, Lebanon and Egypt. Those countries concentrate their criticism against Jews in an attempt divert the focus of the Western world to other hotbeds of tension; thus, they avoid internal criticism about current political regimes.

Those who propagate the myth often ignore the fact that many Americans feel represented by the ethical and moral values defended by Judaism, including the ideals of justice, charity, human dignity and democracy. We recall that, for centuries, the United States has been home to the largest Jewish community in the world outside Israel, whose first members arrived in 1654 to settle there. In the 1930s and 1940s, refugees from Nazism and the European war, Holocaust survivors and Jewish fugitives from Arab countries found shelter in the United States, and blended into the most diverse segments of society. Currently, more than five million Jews live in the United States, many of them in New York, which also houses the second largest synagogue in the world. The Jewish connection to the United States has been going on for many centuries.[190]

---

190 Cited by Bila Sorj, "O Antissemitismo na Europa Hoje", http://www.scielo.br/pdf/nec/n79/05.pdf. Retrieved: June 1, 2018.

Sources

Books

ALVES, Castro. *Vozes da África*. São Paulo, June 11th, 1866.

ALIGHIERI, Dante. *La Divina Comedia*. Translation Luis Martínez de Merlo. Madrid, Catedra, 2001.

ASSUERO, Ludwigsburg, Nast, 1834. Original in German available at Princeton University Library.
http://www.worldcat.org/title/ahasverus/oclc/43074199

BERTRAND, I. *La Franc-Maçonnerie* Sect Juive. Paris, Blound, 1903.

BLOY, Léon. *Le Salut par les Juifs*. Paris, Librairie Adrien Dersay, 1892.

____________. *A Sinagoga Paulista*. 3rd ed. Rio de Janeiro, ABC, 1937.

____________. *Coração de Menino*. Rio de Janeiro, Getúlio M. Costa Editor, 1939.

Os Protocolos dos S·bios de Sião. Coleção Comemorativa do Centenário de Gustavo Barroso. Porto Alegre, Editoria Revisão, 1989, p. 17 (1st reedición 1991).

BAUMAN, Zigmunt. *Life in Fragments: Essays in Postmodern Morality*. Oxford, Blackwell, 1995.

BERTRAND, I. *Maçonaria, Seita Judaica: Suas Origens, Sagacidade e Finalidade Anti-cristãs*, I. ed. 1993. Traducción y Prefacio de Gustavo Barroso, São Paulo, Minerva, 1934.

Catálogo de Propaganda de Livros (n. I), de *A Sementeira*, confiscado y anexado al Pront. N. 581, de la Delegacia Regional de Polícia de Jundiaí, vol. I, Fundo DEOPS/SP. Apesp.

Cartas de Oswaldo Aranha, embaixador do Brasil, embaixador do Brasil nos Estados Unidos, a Getúlio Vargas, presidente do Brasil. Washington, 10.05.1937, 19.05.1937 e 4.6.37, p.2. Pastas OA 37.05.19; OA 37.05.19; e OA 37.06.04/3. CPDOC/RJ.

BLUTEAU, Raphael. *Vocabulàrio Português e Latino, autorizado com exemplo dos melhores escritores portugueses e latinos e offerecido a El Rey de Portugal D. João V*, Coimbra, Real Collegio das Artes da Cia de Jesus., MDCCXIII, pp. 122–134.

CARVALHO, Brasilino de, *O Anti-semitismo de Hitler… E o julgamento Apressado de Alguns Escritores Brasileiros*. Bahia, s.e., 1934.

CUNHA, Euclides da. *À Margem da História*. 5th ed. Porto, Lello & Irmãos, 1941 (1st ed. 1909)

Le Péril Juif: Les Protocoles des Sages de Sion. Paris, Les Nouvelles Editions Nationales, 1934.

DEBRET, Jean-Baptiste. *Viagem Pitoresca e Histórica ao Brasil*. São Paulo, Livraria Martins Fontes, 1940.

DRUMONT, Édouard. *La France Juive*. Paris, Flammarion Éditeur, 1938 (I ed. 1912).

__________. *Le Testament d'un Antisémite*. Paris, E. Dentu Éditeur, 1891.

ESSER, Herman. *Die Jüdische Weltpest*. Múnich, Zentralverlag der NSDAP, 1939.

FELDBERG, Samuel. *Estados Unidos e Israel: uma aliança em questão*. São Paulo, Hucitec, 2008.

FERREIRA, Jerusa Pires. "O Judeu Errante: A Materialidade da Lenda". *Revista Olhar*, Universidade Federal de São Carlos, Año 2, n. 3, 2000, http://www.olhar.ufscar.br/index.php/olhar/article/viewFile/21/20

FIUZA, Mario, *Elucidário das Palavras, Termos e Frases, edição crítica baseada nos manucristos e originais de Viterbo*. 1ed. Lisboa, Livr. Civiliz, 1798/1799.

FRANCHI, Marcelo, "O anti-semitismo é uma doença? A chantagem inaceit·vel", en: *Radio Islam*, http://www.radioislam.org/islam/portugues/antisem/doenca.htm

GOLD, Michael. *Jews Without Money: A Novel, Public Affairs*, 2004, 3rd ed.

GUINET, Edgard. *Ahasvérus*. Paris, Revue de Deux Mondes, 1834.

JANSSEN. J. *Die Allgemeinen Zustände des deutschen Volkes beim Ausgang des Mittelalters*.

LAZARE, Bernard. *L'Antisémitisme: son Histoire et ses Causes*. Paris, Éditions Hean Cres, MCXXXIV.

LIMA, Oswaldo Rocha. *Pedaços do Sertão*. Rio de Janeiro, A. Coelho Branco Filho Editor, 1940.

LUTHER, Martin. *On the Jews and Their Lies*. Cited by Robert Michael, "Luther, Luther Scholars, and the Jews". *Encounter* 46 (n.4): 343–344, 1985.

MARLOWE, Christopher. *El Judío de Malta*. Traducción de Julio César Santoyo. Madrid, Catedra. Cited by ROSA, Maria Eneida Matos da, "A estética da crueldade *em O Judeu de Malta*". Disponible: http://www.pucrs.br/edipucrs/online/vsemanaletras/Artigos%20e%20Notas_PDF/Maria%20Eneida%20Matos%20da%20Rosa.pdf. Consultado el 2/9/2013.

PARIS, Gaston de Bruno Paulin. *Légendes du Moyen Age*, 4. Ed. Paris, Hachette, 1912.

PARIS, Gaston de Bruno Paulin. *Le Juif Errant*, Première Étude. http://www.biblisem.net/etudes/parislje.htm. Consultado el 12/7/2013.

PEREIRA, Manoel Apolinário. *A Vida do Judeu Errante*. Cordel editado por Folheria Luzeiro do Norte do grande poeta João José Silva, s.d., 32 pp. Coleção Ruth Terra, IEB/USP.

PONCINS, Léon de. *Sociétés des Nations Super-état Maçonique*. Paris, Gabriel Beauchesne et fils, MCMXXXVI.

__________. *Les Forces secrètes de la Révolution*. Paris, Brossard, 1928.

__________. *Freemasonry and the Vatican: A Struggle for Recognition*. Britons Publishing, 1968.

PÉRROUX, François. *Les Mythes Hitlériens*. Paris, Librairie générale de droit et de jurisprudence, 1935.

SCHOEBEL, Charles. *La Légende du Juif Érrant*. Paris, 1877.

SIMON, Marcel. *Verus Israel*. Paris, 1948.

"Os judeus e a 'questão racial'", in Radio Islam. Fuente: "Race-Mixing, a bigger threat to people than terrorismo", National Journal, publicado em 13/4/2009.

HIEMER, Ernst, *Der Giftpilz*. Nuremberg, Stürmerverlag, 1938. German Propaganda Archive.

SPRINGMEIER, Fritz, "The Power of the Rostchilds", in: http://rense.com/general77/powers.htm; Reporte "*Jewish 'Control' of the Federal Reserve: A Classic Anti-Semitic Myth.*" Disponible en el sitio de la ADL of http://archive.adl.org/special_reports/control_of_fed/fed_intro.html#.VvQbrvkrLcc, ADL, 2000.

"Judeu Errante". Leyenda narrada en: http://cronicasdeasgardh.blogspot.com.br/2006/05/o-judeu-errante.html

Cartel de la exposición *Der ewige Jude* (El judio errante). Múnich, 8 de noviembre de 1937.

Der ewige Jude, Ein dokumentarischer Film der D. F. G. Musik: Franz R. Friedl

PRANAITIS, I. B. [Reverendo]. "El Talmud Desenmascarado". http://holywar.org/Pranaitis_El-Talmud-desenmascarado.pdf

SUE, Eugène. *Le Juif Errant*. Paris, 1845.

Official Letters

Misiva de Muniz de Aragão, Embajador de Brasil en Berlín a Oswaldo Aranha, ministro de Relaciones Exteriores. Berlín, 26 de abril de 1938. Ref, 511.14 (193). AHI/RJ.

Misiva de Hildebrando Accioly, Secretario General, a Oswaldo Aranha, Ministro de Relaciones Exteriores. Rio de Janeiro, 22/4/1938, pp. 3–4. *Ofícios Recebidos*, abril de 1938. AHI.

Periodicals

O Campineiro, 10 de abril de 1849. São Paulo, Typografia Liberal, 1849. Biblioteca J. Mindlin/USP-SP.

Revista *Careta*. Rio de Janeiro, n. 1558, abril de 1938 [portada]; n. 1591, dic. 1938 [portada]. B.M.M.A./SP.

Revista *Careta*. Rio de Janeiro, n. 1470, ago. 1936, p. 39; n. 1460, jun. 1936; n. 439, jan. 1936, p.31; n. 1449, mar. 1936, p.34; n. 1467, ago. 1936, p. 19; n. 1555, abr. 1938, portada; n. 1558, abr. 1938, portada; n. 1561, mayo, 1938, portada; n. 1477, oct. 1936, portada; n. 1580, oct. 1938, p. 37. B.M.M.A/SP.

Diário do Rio de Janeiro, 5 de diciembre de 1845.

General Bibliography

ANDRIÈS, Lise. *Le Grand Livre des Secrets – Le Colportage em France aux 17e et 18e siècles,* Paris, Éditions Imago, 1994.

ANDERSON, Benedict. *Imagined Communities: Reflections on the Origins and Spread of Nationalism.* New York, Verso Books, 2006.

ALCALA, Angel (org.). *Judíos, Sefarditas, Conversos. La expulsión de 1492 y sus consecuencias.* New York/Madrid, Ed. Ámbito, 1992.

APPEL, John; Appel, Selma. *Comics da Imigração na América.* Trad. Sérgio Roberto Souza. São Paulo, Perspectiva, 1994.

ARENDT, Hannah. *Los Orígenes del Totalitarismo.* Madrid, Alianza Editorial, 2006.

ARRIBAS, Javier Domínguez Arribas, *El Enemigo Judeu-masónico en la Propaganda Franquista (1936–1945),* Madrid, Marcial Pons Editorial, 2009

ATAIDE, Maria das Graças; ATAIDE, Rosário. *História (nem sempre) bem-humorada de Pernambuco.* Vol. I. Recife, Ediçıes Bagaço, 1999.

ATTALI, Jacques. *Les juifs, le monde et l'argent.* Paris, Le Livre de Poche, 2003.

BAUDELAIRE, Charles. "De l'essence du rire et généralement du comique dans les arts plastiques" (1885). In: LEMAITRE, Henri (ed.). *Curiosités Esthétiques.* Paris, Garnier, 1986.

BOSI, Alfredo. *Dialética da Colonização.* São Paulo, Companhia das Letras, 1992.

CARNEIRO, Maria Luiza Tucci. *Cidadão do Mundo. O Brasil diante do Holocausto e dos Refugiados do Nazifascismo*. São Paulo, Perspectiva, 2011.

________. *Preconceito Racial em Portugal e Brasil Colônia – O Mito da Pureza de Sangue contra os Cristãos-novos, Séculos XVI ao XIX*. 3rd ed. São Paulo, Perspectiva, 2004.

________. (org). *O Anti-semitismo nas Américas. História e Memória*. Prefácio de Pilar Rahola. São Paulo, Edusp, 2007.

COHN, Norman, *The Pursuit of the Millenium: Revolutionary Millenarians and Mystical Anarchists of the Middle Ages*. London and New York, Oxford University Press, 1970.

________. *El Mito de la Conspiración Judía Mundial: Los Protocolos de los Sabios de Sion*. Madrid, Alianza Editorial, 1983.

COLOMBO, Eduardo. *El Imaginario Social*. Traducción de Bernard Weigel. Montevideo/Buenos Aires, Editorial Altamira/Editorial Nordan-Comunidad, 1993.

CONNELLY, John. *From Enemy to Brother: The Revolution in Catholic Teaching on the Jews*. Cambridge, MA, Harvard University Press, 2012.

CORDEIRO, Carlos (org.). *Autoritarismos, Totalitarismos, e Respostas Democráticas*. Coimbra: CEIS20. Ponta Delgada, Centro de Estudos Gaspar Frutuoso da Universidade de Açores, 2011.

CROCI, Federico; CARNEIRO, Maria Luiza Tucci (orgs.). *Tempos de Fascismos*. São Paulo, Edusp, Imprensa Oficial, Arquivo Público do Estado, 2011.

CUNHA, Celso da. *Educação e Autoritarismo no Estado Novo*. São Paulo, Cortez, 1981.

ECO, Umberto. *Sei passeggiate nei boschi narrativi*. Milano, Bompiani, 2000.

EWEN, Frederic. Brecht. *Sua Vida, Sua Arte, Seu Tempo*. São Paulo, Editora Globo, 1991.

FLANNERY, Edward. *The Anguish of the Jews: Twenty-Three Centuries of Antisemitism*. New Jersey: Paulist Press, 2004, 2nd ed.

FONTETTE, François de. *Histoire de l'Antisémitisme*. Paris, Presses Universitaires de France. Col Que sais-je?, 2015

GIRARDET, Raoul. *Mythes et Mythologies Politiques*. Paris, Seuil, 1990.

GORENSTEIN, Lina; CARNEIRO, Maria Luiza Tucci (orgs.). *Ensaios sobre a Intolerância. Inquisição, Marranismo e Anti-Semitismo*. São Paulo, Humanitas/FAPESP, 2002.

ISAAC, Jules. *Las Raíces Cristianas del Antisemitismo*. Buenos Aires, Paidos, 1966.

KAISERLING, Meyer. *História dos Judeus em Portugal*. São Paulo, Pioneira, 1971.

KAMPMANN, Wanda. *Deutsche und Juden – Die Geschichte der Juden in Deutschland conm Mittelalter bis zum Beginn des Ersten Weltkrieges*. Frankfurt, M. Fischer, 1979.

KOSSOY, Boris. *Realidades e Ficções na Trama Fotográfica*, 2nd ed. São Paulo, Ateliê Editorial, 2001.

LIMA, Rossini Tavares de. *Folclore das Festas Cíclicas*. Rio de Janeiro, Irmãos Vitale Editores, 1971.

LIPOVETSKY, Gilles. *Métamorphoses de la culture libérale: éthique, médias, entreprise*. Montréal, Éditions Liber, 2002.

LOPES, Hélio. *Letras de Minas e Outros Ensaios*. São Paulo, Edusp, 1997.

MARTINS, Wilson. *História da Inteligência Brasileira*. Vol. III: (1855–1877). São Paulo, Cultrix/Edusp, 1977.

MASSENZIO, Marcello. *La Passion selon le Juif Errant*. Traducido del italiano al francés por Patrice Cotensin. Paris, L'Echoppe, 2006.

MEYER, Marlyse. *Folhetim, Uma História*. São Paulo, Companhia das Letras, 1996.

MINOIS, Georges. *Histoire du rire et de la dérision*. Paris, Fayard, 2000.

MONTEIRO, Yara Nogueira. *Da Maldição Divina à Exclusão Social: Um Estudo da Hanseníase em São Paulo*. Tese de Doutorado em História Social, Departamento de História, FFLCH, Universidade de São Paulo, 1995.

MONTEIRO, Yara Nogueira; CARNEIRO, Maria Luiza Tucci (orgs.). *As Doenças e os Medos Sociais*. São Paulo, Editora Unifesp, 2013.

MORAIS, Vamberto. *Pequena História do Anti-semitismo*. São Paulo, Difel, 1972.

MOTA, Ático Vilas-Boas da. *Queimação de Judas: Catarismo, Inquisição e Judeus no Folclore Brasileiro*. Rio de Janeiro, MEC; SEAC; Funarte; Instituto Nacional do Folclore, 1981.

NOVINSKY, Anita. *Cristãos-novos na Bahia*. São Paulo, Perspectiva, 1972.

PERROUX, François. *Les Mythes Hitlériens*. Paris, Librairie générale de droit et de jurisprudence, 1935.

POLIAKOV, Léon. *Du Christ aux Juifs de Cour* (Histoire de l'Antisémitisme). Paris, Calmann-Lévy, 1955).

_________. *La Causalité Diaboloque: Essai sur l'origine des persécutions*. Paris, Calmann-Lévy, 1994. Collection Liberté d'Esprit.

_________. *Le Mythe Aryen: Essai sur les sources du racisme et les nationalismes*. Paris, Calmann-Lévy, 1994. Collection Liberté d'Esprit.

RENONCIAT, Annie. *La Vie et l'Oeuvre de Gustave Doré*. Paris, ACR Éditions, 1983. (343 illustrations).

ROBERTS, John. *Mythology of Secret Societies*. London, Secker & Warburg, 1972.

ROTH, Cecil. *A Short History of the Jewish People*. London, Hartmore House, 1969.

_________. *A History of the Marranos*. New York, Meridian Books/The Jewish Publication Society of America, 1959.

SARAIVA, Antonio José. *Inquisição e Cristãos-novos*. Porto, Inova, 1969.

SEAVER, James Everett. *The Persecution of the Jews in the Roman Empire (300–428)*. Lawrence, Kansas, University of Kansas, 1952.

SELTZER, Robert M. *Jewish People, Jewish Thought: The Jewish Experience in History*. London, Pearson, 1980.

SICROF, Albert. *Les Controvers des Status de Pureté de* Sang en Espagne du XVe au XVIIe siécle. Paris, Libraire Marcel Didier, 1960.

STALLAERT, Christiane. *Etnogénesis y Etnicidad en España. Una aproximación histórico-antropológica al casticismo*, Barcelona, Proyecto a Ediciones, 1998.

TAGUIEFF, Pierre-André. *Les Protocoles des Sages de Sion. Introduction à l'Étude des des Protocoles: un faux et ses usages dans le siécles. 2 vols.* Paris, Berg International, 1992.

TILLIER, Bertrand. *À la Charge! La Caricature en France de 1789 à 2000*. Paris, Les Éditions de l'Amateur, 2005.

TRACHTENBERG, Joshua. *El Diablo y los Judíos. La concepción medieval del judio y su relación con el antisemitismo moderno.* Buenos Aire, Editorial Paidos, 1975.

WEBB, James. *The Age of the Irrational: The Flight from Reason – I.* London, 1971.

___________. *The Occult Establishment.* La Salle, 1977, vol. II.

WEBER, Max. *La ética protestante y el espíritu del capitalismo.* Madrid, Alianza Editorial, 2012.

WINOCK, Michel. *La France et les Juifs, de 1789 à nos Jours*. Paris, Éditions du Seuil, 2004.

WOLFF, Egon e Frieda. *Os Judeus no Brasil Imperial.* São Paulo, Centro de Estudos Judaicos/FFLCH-USP, 1975.

SOMBART, Werner. *El Apogeo del Capitalismo*. México, Fondo de Cultura Económica, 1984, 2 vol.

TORGAL, Luis Reis; PAULO, Heloisa (orgs.). *Estados Autoritários e Totalitários e suas Representações.* Coimbra, Imprensa da Universidade de Coimbra, 2008.

VIDAL-NAQUET, Pierre. *Les Assassins de la mémoire. Un "Eichmann de papier" et d'autres essais sur le révisionisme*. Paris, Seuil, 1995.

Articles

ALCALA, Angel. "Marranes: Le judaïsme laïque dans le nouveaux monde". In: ROSEMAN, I. (org.). *Juifs laïques, du réligieux vers le culturel.* Paris, Corlet, 1992, pp. 92–96.

ANSART, Pierre, "Ideologías, conflitos y poder". In: COLOMBO, Eduardo. *El Imaginario Social.* Traducción de Bernardo Weigel. Montevideo/Buenos Aires, Editorial Altamira/Editorial Nordan-Comunidad, 1993, pp. 101–102.

FERNANDES, Cristiane Soares, "Resenha: Análise dos conceitos fundamentais apresentados no Cap. 4 – Bosques Possíveis, do livro Seis Passeios pelos Bosques da Ficção, de Umberto Eco." http://pt.scribd.com/doc/23998943/Analise-do-livro-Seis-Passeios-pelos-Bosques-da-Ficcao-Umberto-Eco.

FERREIRA, Jerusa Pires. "O Judeu Errante: A Materialidade da Lenda". *Revista Olhar*/Centro de Educação e Ciências Humanas da UFSC, vol. 2, n. 3, mayo–junio, 2000, p. 25.

"EUA denunciam a escalada de ódio contra judeus e muçulmanos". In: *Portal Terra,* 20 de mayo de 2013. http://noticias.terra.com.br/mundo/estados-unidos/eua-denunciam-escalada-do-odio-contra-judeus-e-muculmanos,4dcaaa33a92ce310VgnCLD2000000ec6eb0aRCRD.html

CAMATI, Anna Stegh. "O Mercador de Veneza de Michel Radford: Adaptação, Historicização e Interpolação". In: CORSEUIL, Anelise Reich et al. (orgs.). *Ensaios de Literatura, Teatro e Cinema.* Florianópolis, Fundação Cultural Badesc/Cultura Inglesa, 2013.

CONNELLY, John. "Converts who Changed the Church". In: *Forward,* 30/7/2012. http://forward.com/opinion/159955/converts-who-changed-the-church/

CREUTZ, W. "A Autenticidade dos Protocolos dos Sábios de Sião". Os *Protocolos dos Sábios de Sião.* Coleção Comemorativa do Centenário de Gustavo Barroso. Porto Alegre, Revisão, 1989.

DANIELE, Ariel. "Nada de Novo: É o próprio Bergoglio a confirmar-se herege!". *ProRoma.* Mariana, 30 de dezembro de

2013. http://promariana.wordpress.com/2013/12/30/nada-de-novo-e-o-proprio-bergoglio-a-confirmar-se-herege/

FELDBERG, Samuel. Enero 2007. https://www.researchgate.net/publication/33760849_Estados_Unidos_da_America_e_Israel_uma_alianca_em_questao

FELDBERG, Samuel. 10/9/2013. https://coletivojudaico.wordpress.com/category/centro-de-cultura-judaica/page/2/

FELDMAN, Sérgio Alberto. "Deicida e Aliado: O Judeu na Patrística". Academia.edu. http://www.academia.edu/1375074/Deicida_e_aliado_do_demonio_o_judeu_na_Patristica

FEROLLA, Vítor Carvalho. "Existem Judeus Pobres". *Israel Today News*. www.thegreatcommandment.com/2008/existem-judeus-pobres.html

FROESE, Arno. "A Mais Perigosa Forma de Ódio aos Judeus: os Árabes Adotam Mitos Anti-semitas Europeus". *Revista Notícias de Israel*, agosto de 2013.

GORDON, Peter E. "The Border Crossers". *New Republic*, 18 de mayo de 2012; http://www.newrepublic.com/article/books-and-arts/magazine/103331/catholic-jewish-anti-semitism-pope-vatican-nazis

GRAHAM, Billy [Reverendo]. "Billy Graham Screens 'The Passion of the Christ'". In: *WND*, 26/11/2003, http://www.wnd.com/2003/11/22003/

KLIKSBERG, Bernardo. "A Comunidade Judaica da Argentina em Perigo". *Morashá*, edición 36, marzo de 2002. Enlace: http://www.morasha.com.br/judaismo-no-mundo/a-comunidade-judaica-da-argentina-em-perigo.html. Consultado el 5/7/2013.

MACNEIL, Jr., Donald G. "As Epidemias e os Bodes Expiatórios". Cuaderno "The New York Times", *Folha de S. Paulo*, 14 de setiembre de 2009.

NOBLAT, Ricardo. "Fatos e Fotos e Manchete". Cited by CURAN, Mark. *História do Brasil em Cordel*. São Paulo, Edusp, 2001, pp. 24–25.

NOVINSKY, Anita. "Consideraciones sobre los criptojudíos hispano-portugueses. El caso de Brasil". In: HANSAN-GOKEN, Galit. "*Le Juif Errant est Revenu*". Commissaire de l'exposition Laurence Sigal-Klagsbald, Musée d'Art et d'Histoire du Judaïsme, 2001.

PARADISO, S. R. "Shakespeare: Anti-semita? A Imagem do Judeu em O Mercador de Veneza". *Revista Cesumar*. Ciências Humanas e Sociais Aplicadas, Maringá, vol. 13, n. I, 2008, p. 115.

PEREIRA, Kenia Maria de Alemida. "O Judeu Errante nas Minas Gerais: Carlos Drummond de Andrade em Busca de Ahasverus". Arquivo Maaravi. *Revista Digital de Estudos Judaicos da UFMG*, Belo Horizonte, vol. 7, n. 13, octubre de 2013.

RAHOLA, Pilar. "Judíos de seis brazos". Conferencia de la periodista en el *Global Forum for Combating Antisemitism*, 16/12/2009. Disponible en el sitio de la autora, http://www.pilarrahola.com/3_0/CONFERENCIAS/default.cfm?ID=1775

SANTOS, Celi Barbosa dos; PARADISO, Sílvio Ruiz. "A Imagem do Judeu na Literatura Britânica: Shylock, Barrabás e Gafin". *Diálogos & Saberes*, Mandaguari, vol. 8, n. i, 2012, pp. 213–231.

SAUVAGET, Bernadette. "Le Juif Errant est Revenu". *La Vie*, n. 2931, 31 de octubre de 2001, http://www.lavie.fr/archives/2001/10/31/le-juif-errant-est-revenu,3789703.php

SORJ, Bila. "Anti-semitismo na Europa Hoje". *Novos Estudos – Cebrap*, n. 79. São Paulo, noviembre de 2007. http://www.scielo.br/scielo.php?script=sci_arttext&pid=S0101-33002007000300005

STORCH, Moisés. "A Satanização dos Estados Unidos e de Israel e a Manipulação do Sofrimento Palestino", 20 de setiembre de 2001, *Paz e Agora*, http://www.pazagora.org/2001/09/a-satanizacao-dos-estados-unidos-e-de-israel-e-a-manipulacao-do-sofrimento-palestino/

VENCESLAU, Paulo de Tarso; FREIRE, Alípio. Entrevista "Jacob Gorender", *Revista Teoria e Debate*, edición 11, 1 de julio de 1990, http://www.teoriaedebate.org.br/materias/nacional/jacob-gorender

WEITMAN, Rabino Y. David. "Introdução: O Significado Profundo da Dispersão e das Migrações do Povo Judeu". *Recordações da Imigração Judaica em S. Paulo*. São Paulo, Maayanot, 2013, pp. 9–18.

Reference Works

Dicionário Histórico-Biográfico Brasileiro. Coord. Israel Beloch & Alzira Alves de Abreu, Rio de Janeiro, Forense Universitária, CPDOC/FGV, Finep, 1985, vol. I.

O'BRIEN, Joanne & PALME, Martin. Atlas das Religiões. São Paulo, Publifolha, 2009.

Dicionário Exegético, por hum Anônymo, Lisboa, Officina Patriarcal de Franc. Ameno, 1781.

Thesis and Dissertations

LUZ, Enrique. *O Eterno Judeu: Anti-semitismo e Antibolchevismo nos Cartazes de Propaganda Política Nacional-Socialista (1919–1945)*. Disertación de Maestría em Historia de la Facultad de Filosofía y Ciencias Humanas de la Universidad Federal de Minas Gerais, UFMG, Brasil.

SOUZA, Maurini de. *A Trajetória do Tratamento de Segunda Pessoa em Textos Publicitários durante o Século XX: Um Estudo Comparativo entre Brasil e Alemanha*. Tesis de Doctorado, Programa de Posgrado em Estudios Lingüísticos del sector de Ciencias Humanas, Letras y Artes. Curitiba, Universidad Federal de Paraná, 2012. http://dspace.c3sl.ufpr.br/dspace/bitstream/handle/1884/26951/VERSAO%20FINAL.pdf?sequence=1

Websites

http://www.arqshoah.com
https://collections.ushmm.org/search/
http://www.kdfrases.com/frase/91297
http://www.pilarrahola.com
https://radioislam.org/islam/spanish/index.htm
http://www.catolicosalerta.com.ar/masoneria/contra-iglesia.pdf

Videos/Dailymotion

"Sionistas controlam a mídia no Brasil" http://www.dailymotion.com/video/xyvq8v_sionistas-controlam-a-midia-do-brasil-israelitas-falsos-judeus-asquenazitas-jafetitas_animals;

"Os protocolos dos sábios de sião": http://www.dailymotion.com/video/xyvu7u_os-protocolos-dos-sabios-de-siao-parte-7-de-7-nova-ordem-mundial-e-religioes_animals

Onomastic Index

Index of Contents

The Author

Historian and Associate Professor at the Department of History, FFLCH, University of São Paulo (USP), Maria Luiza Tucci Carneiro is accredited in the following Graduate Programs: Social History (FFLCH/USP), Human Rights (São Francisco School of Law/USP), and Hebrew and Arabic Language (FFLCH/USP). Coordinator of LEER – Laboratory of Studies on Ethnicity, Racism and Discrimination of the Department of History, where she is developing the project *Arqshoah* – Virtual Archive on the Holocaust and Antisemitism.

Authored books: *Cidadão do Mundo. O Brasil diante do Holocausto e dos Refugiados do Nazifascismo*, 1938–1948 (Perspectiva, 2011). Published in German by LIT Verlag with the title, *Weltbürger. Brasilien und die Jüdischen Flüchtlinge 1933–1948* (translation Marlen Eckl); *Brasil Judaico, Mosaico de Nacionalidades* (Maayanot, 2013); *Preconceito Racial em Portugal e Brasil Colônia. Os Cristãos-novos e o Mito da Pureza de Sangue* (3rd ed., Perspectiva, 2005); *O Anti-semitismo na Era Vargas, Fantasmas de uma Geração* (3rd ed., Perspectiva, 2001); *Brasil, Refúgio nos Trópicos. A Trajetória das Judeus Refugiados do Nazi-fascismo* (Estação Liberdade, 1997); *Livros Proibidos, Ideias Malditas* (2nd ed., Ateliê Editorial, 2002); *O Veneno da Serpente,*

Reflexões sobre o Moderno Anti-semitismo no Brasil (Perspectiva, 2003); *Holocausto. Crime contra a Humanidade* (Ática, 2000); *O Racismo na História do Brasil: Mito e Realidade* (8th ed., Ática, 1999).

Authored collections: *Olhares de Liberdade: CIP, Espaço de Resistência e Memória* (CIP 2018); *100 Anos do Genocídio Armênio,* with Carlos Boucualt and Heitor Loureiro (Humanitas, 2019); *Índios no Brasil: Vida, Cultura e Morte,* with Miriam Rossi; *Recordações dos Primórdios da Imigração Judaica em S. Paulo* (Maayanot, 2013); *As Doenças e os Medos Sociais,* with Yara Monteiro (UNIFEST, 2012); *Tempos de Fascismos,* with Federico Croci (Edusp; Arquivo Público do Estado, Imesp, 2009); *Imigrantes Japoneses no Brasil,* with Marcia Yumi Takeuchi (Edusp; Fapesp, 2008); *O Anti-semitismo nas Américas. História e Memória* (Edusp, 2008, 684 pp.); *Minorias Silenciadas: História da Censura no Brasil* (2nd ed., Edusp, Fapesp, 2002); *Ensaios sobre a Intolerância. Inquisição, Marranismo e Antisemitismo,* with Lina Gorenstein (Humanitas, 2002).